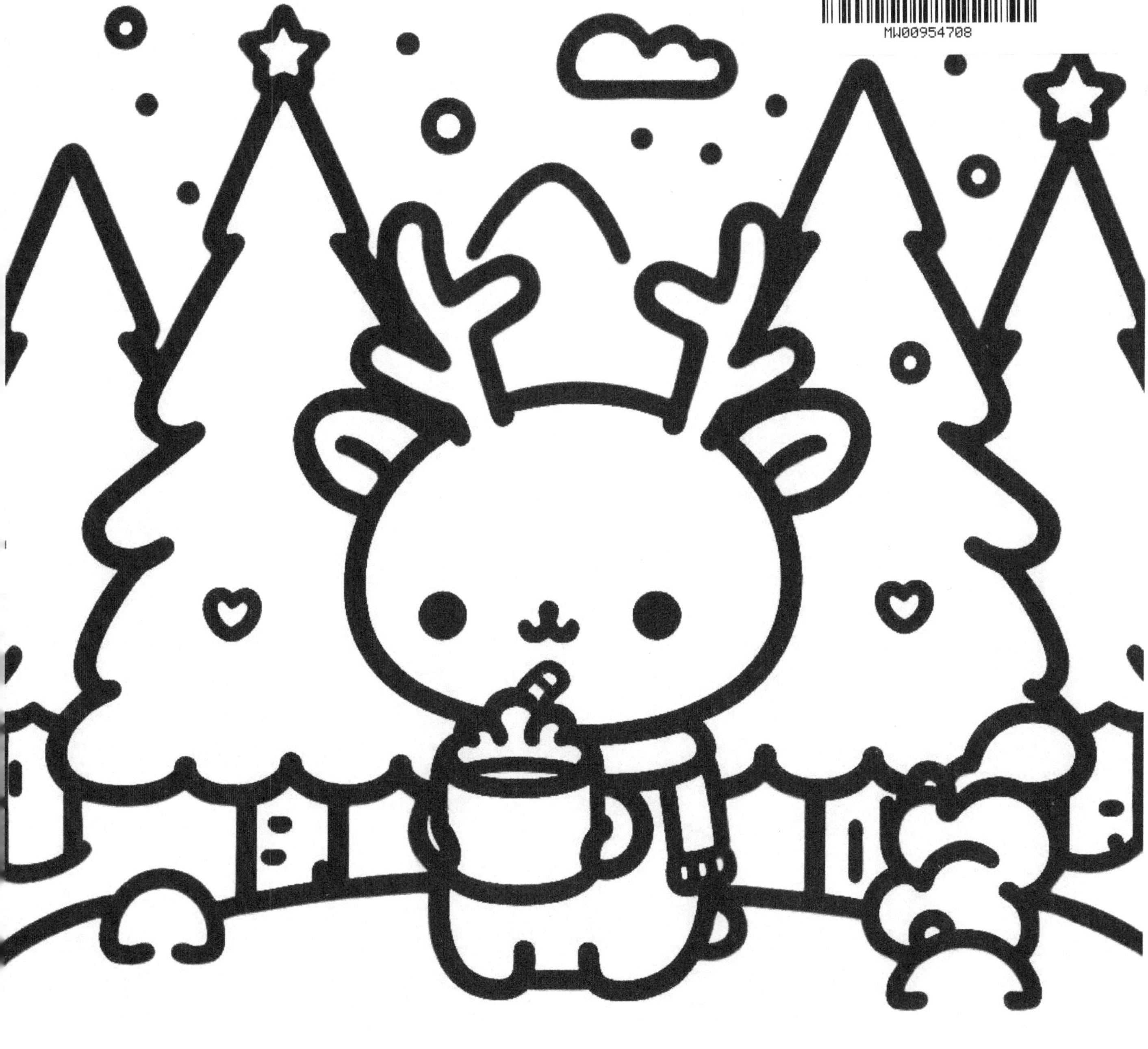

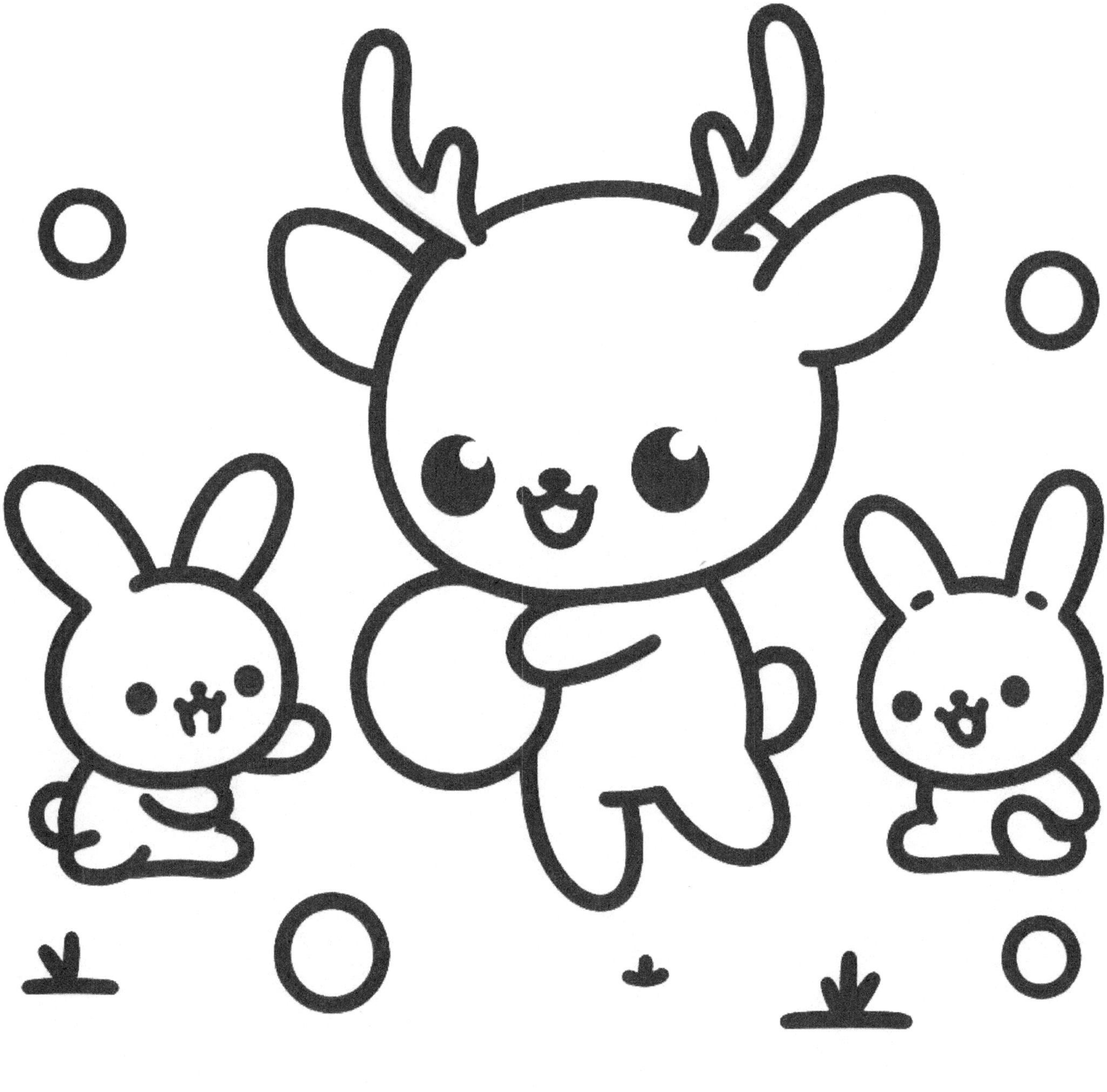

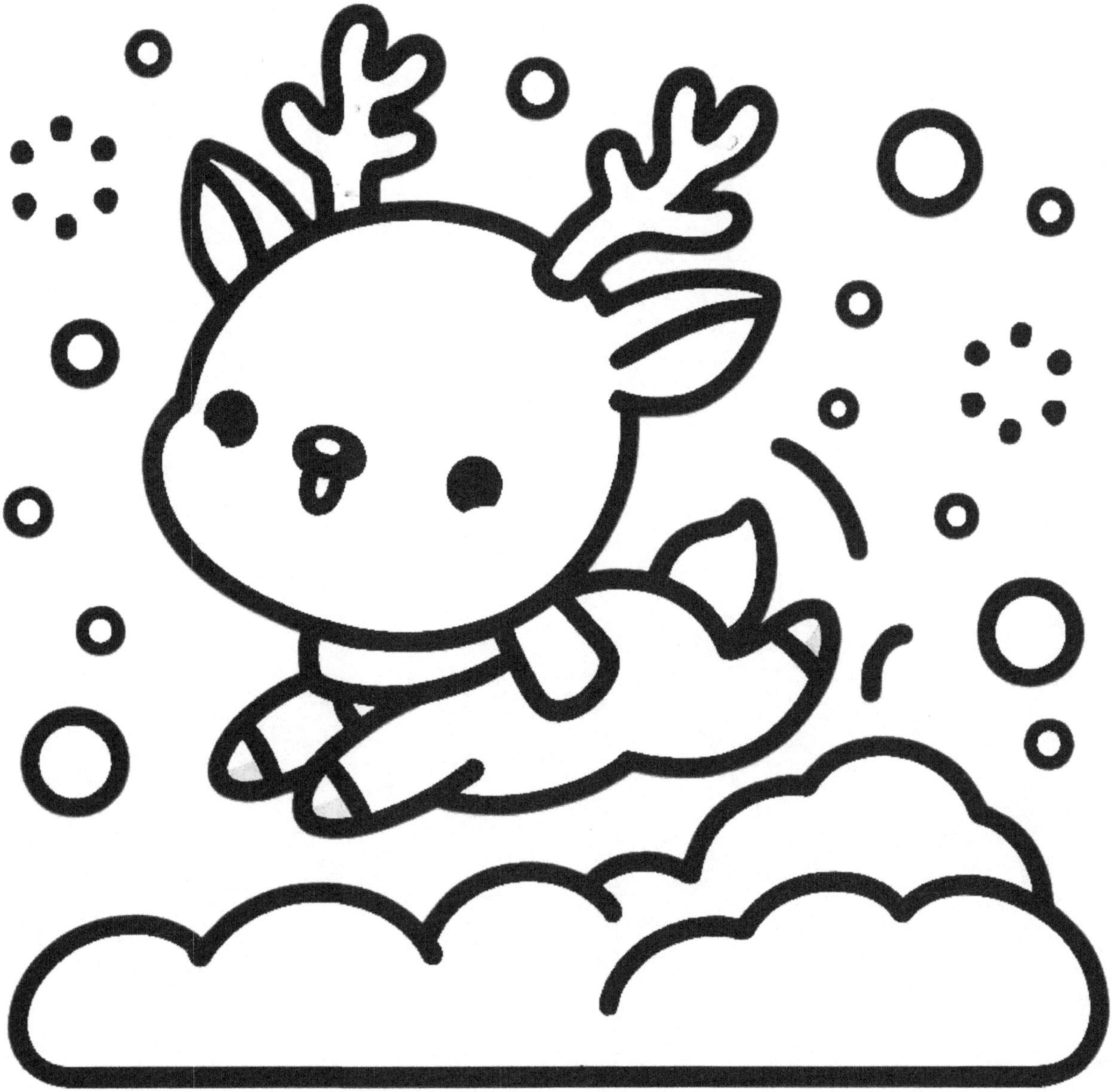

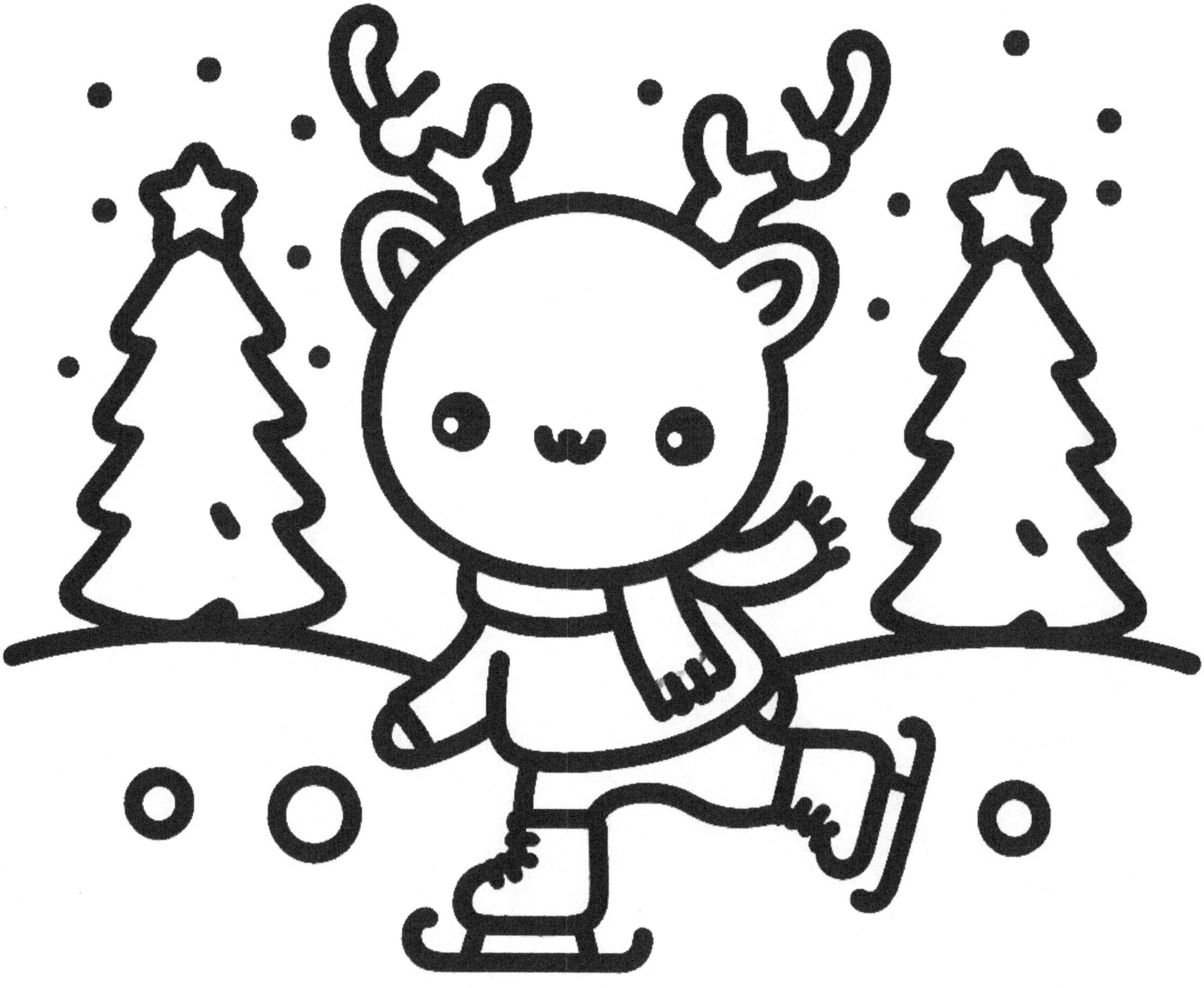

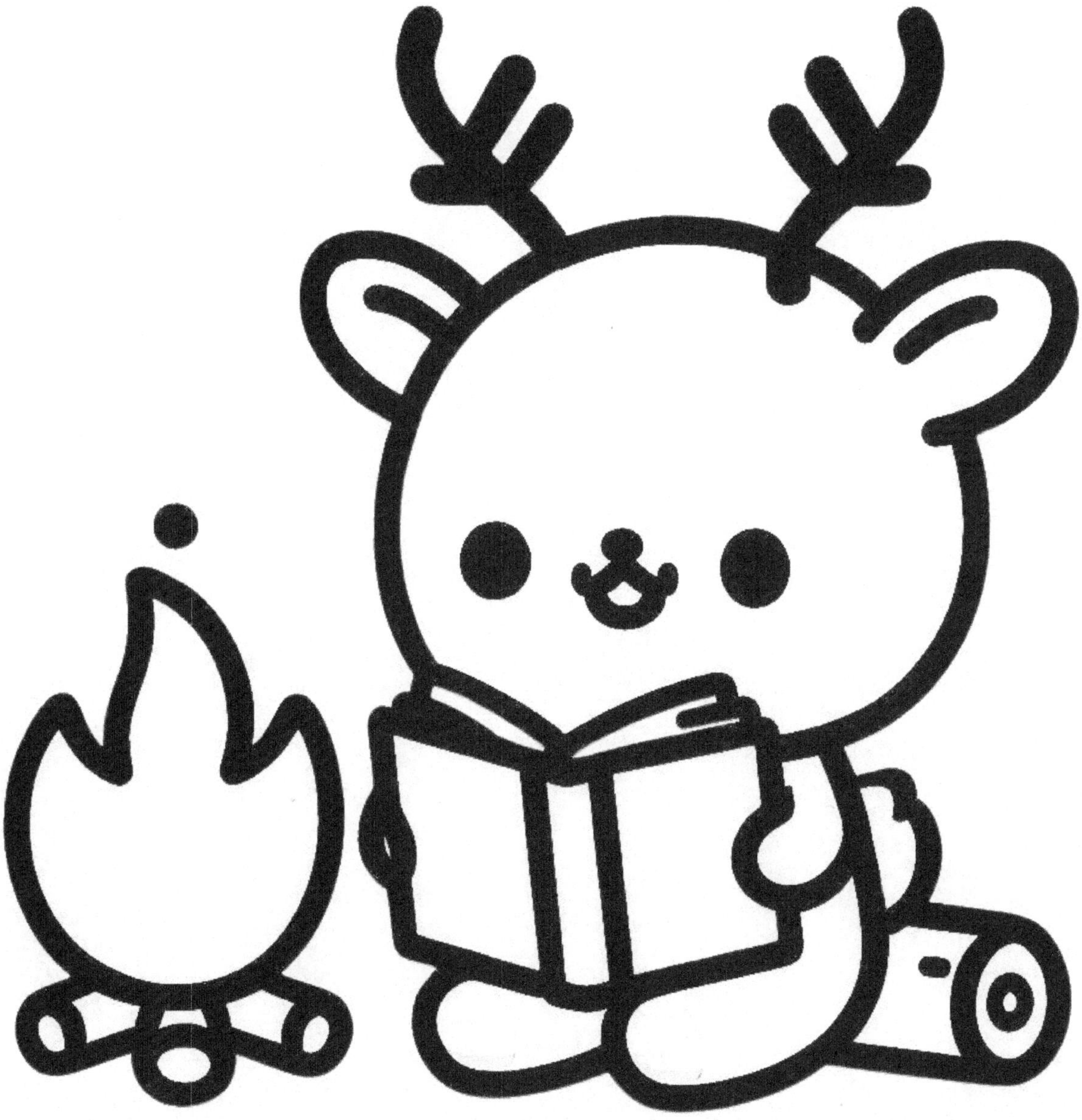

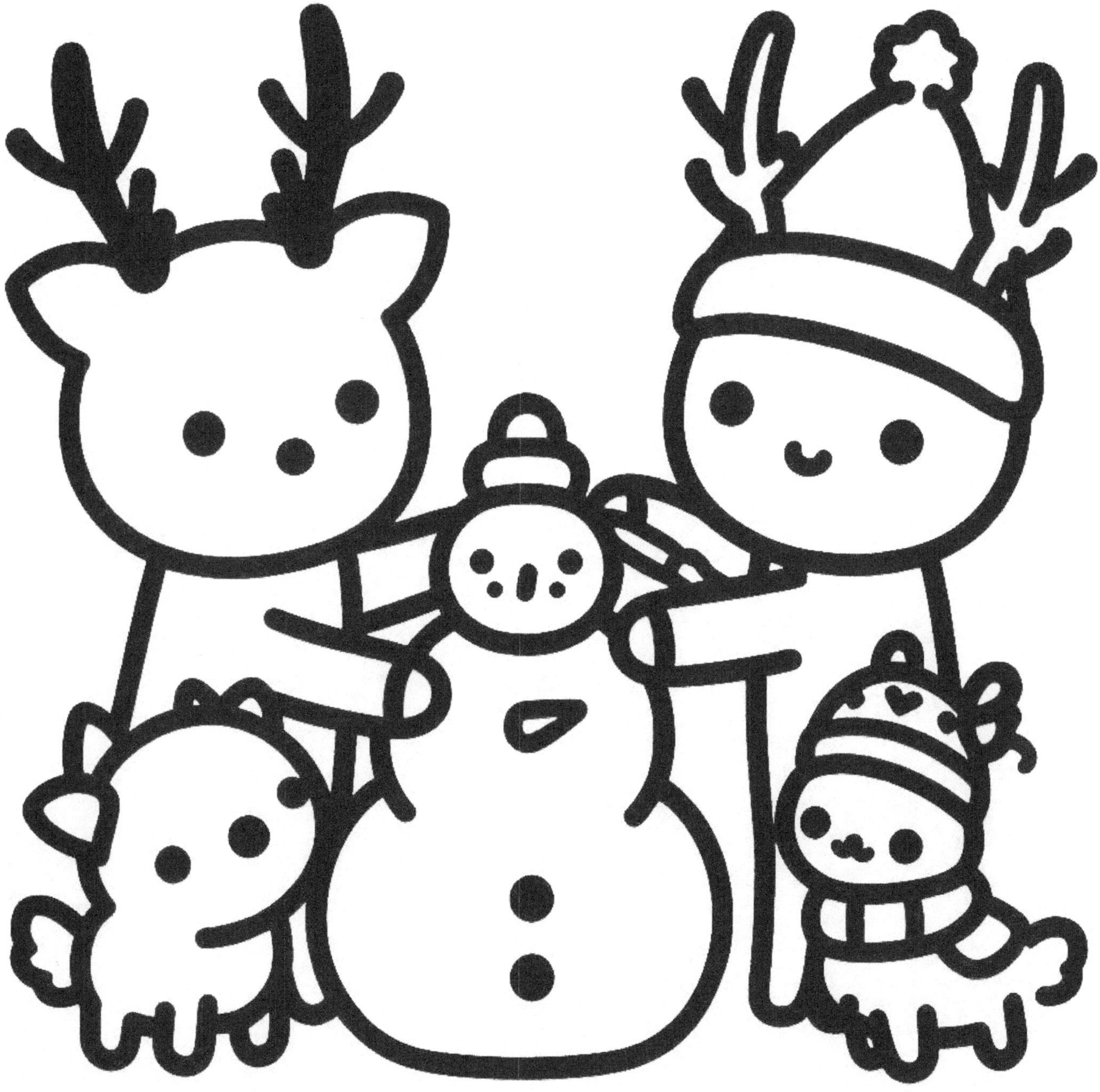

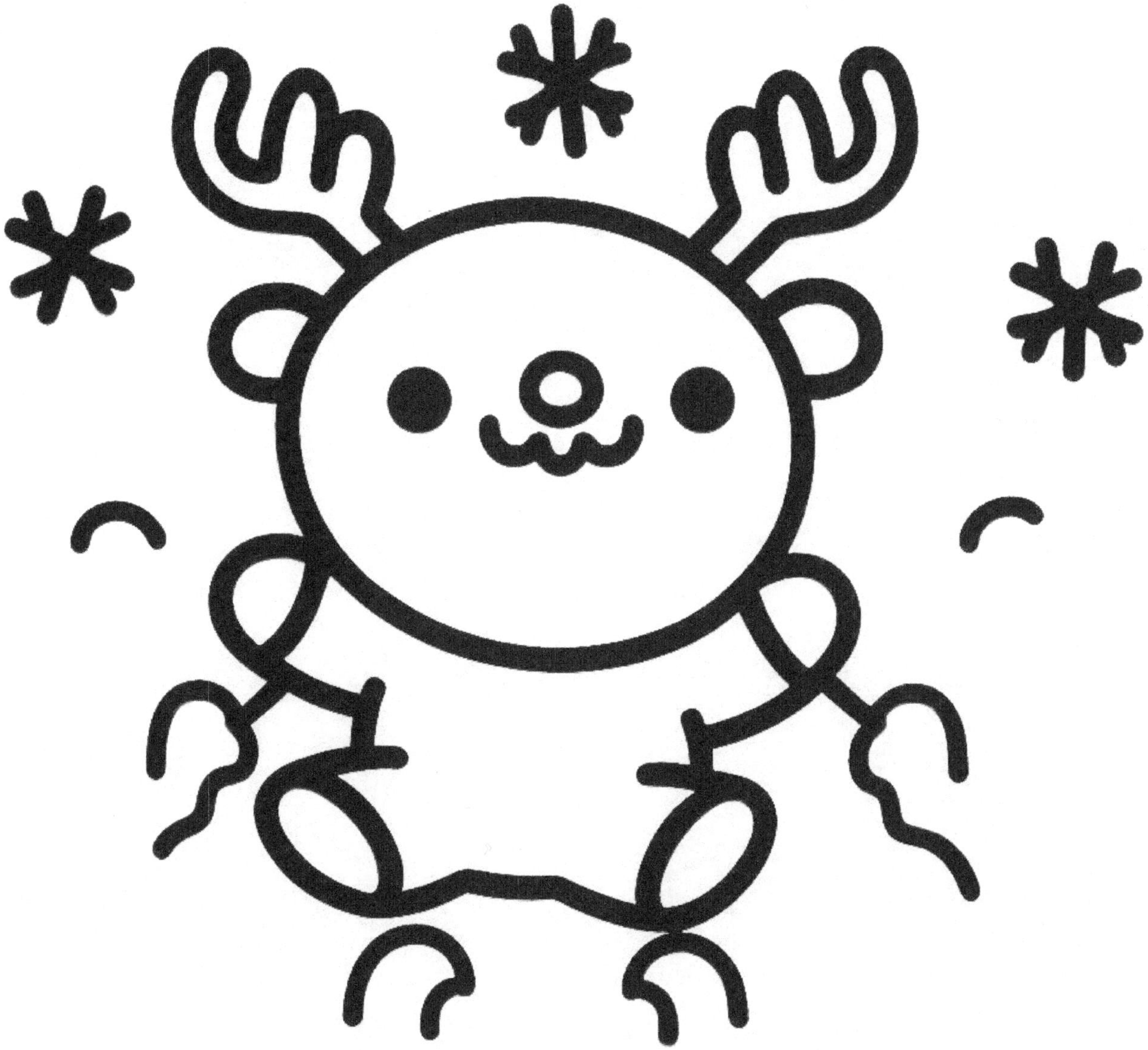

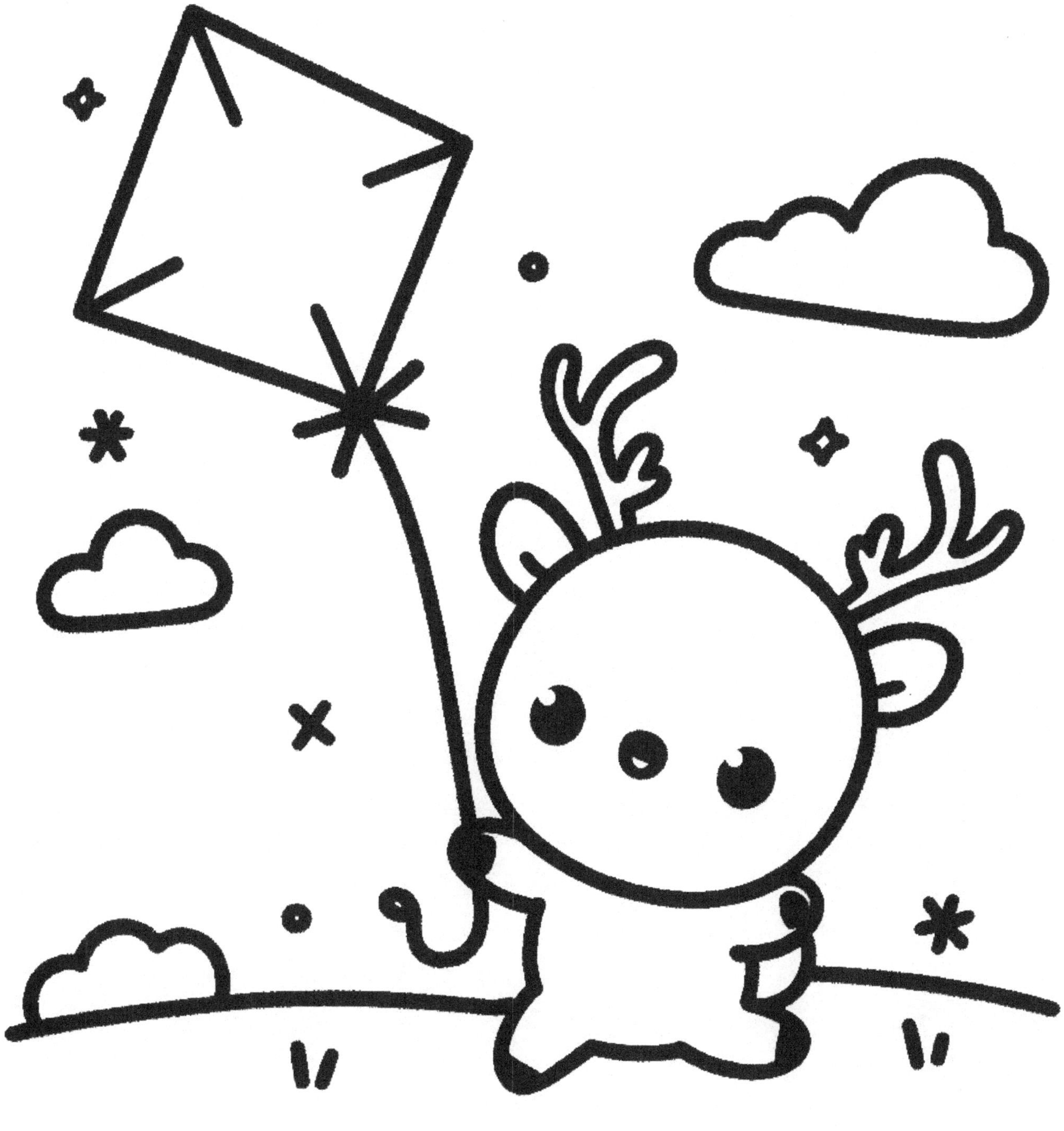

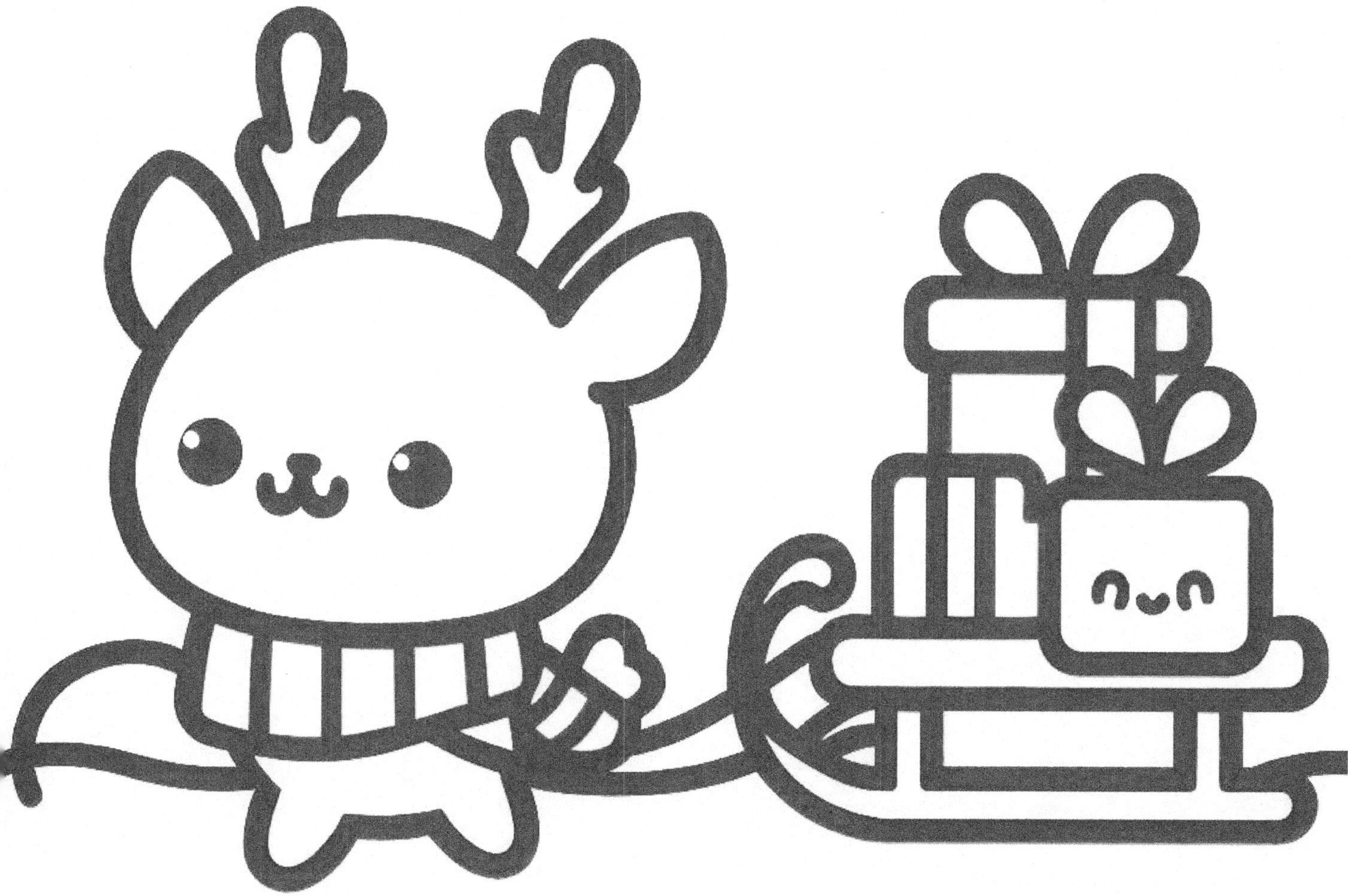

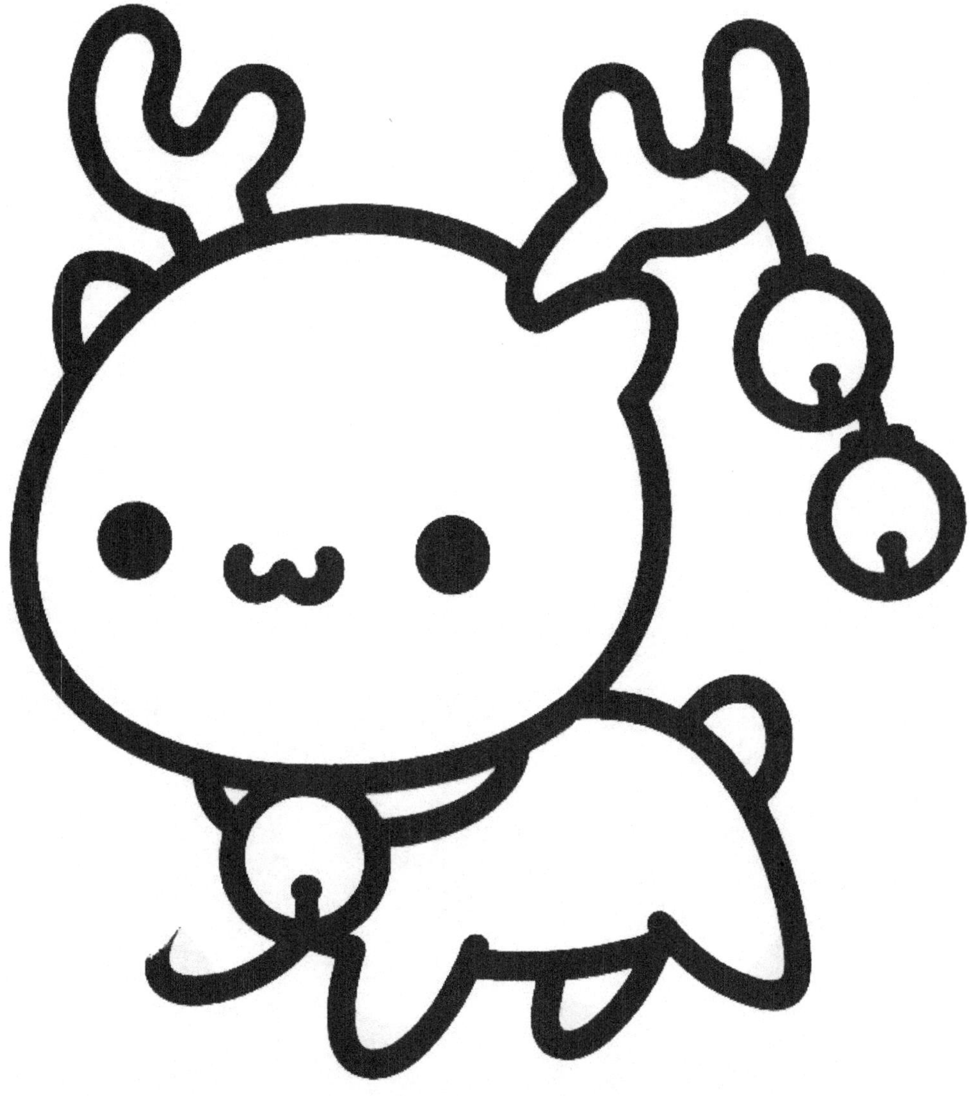

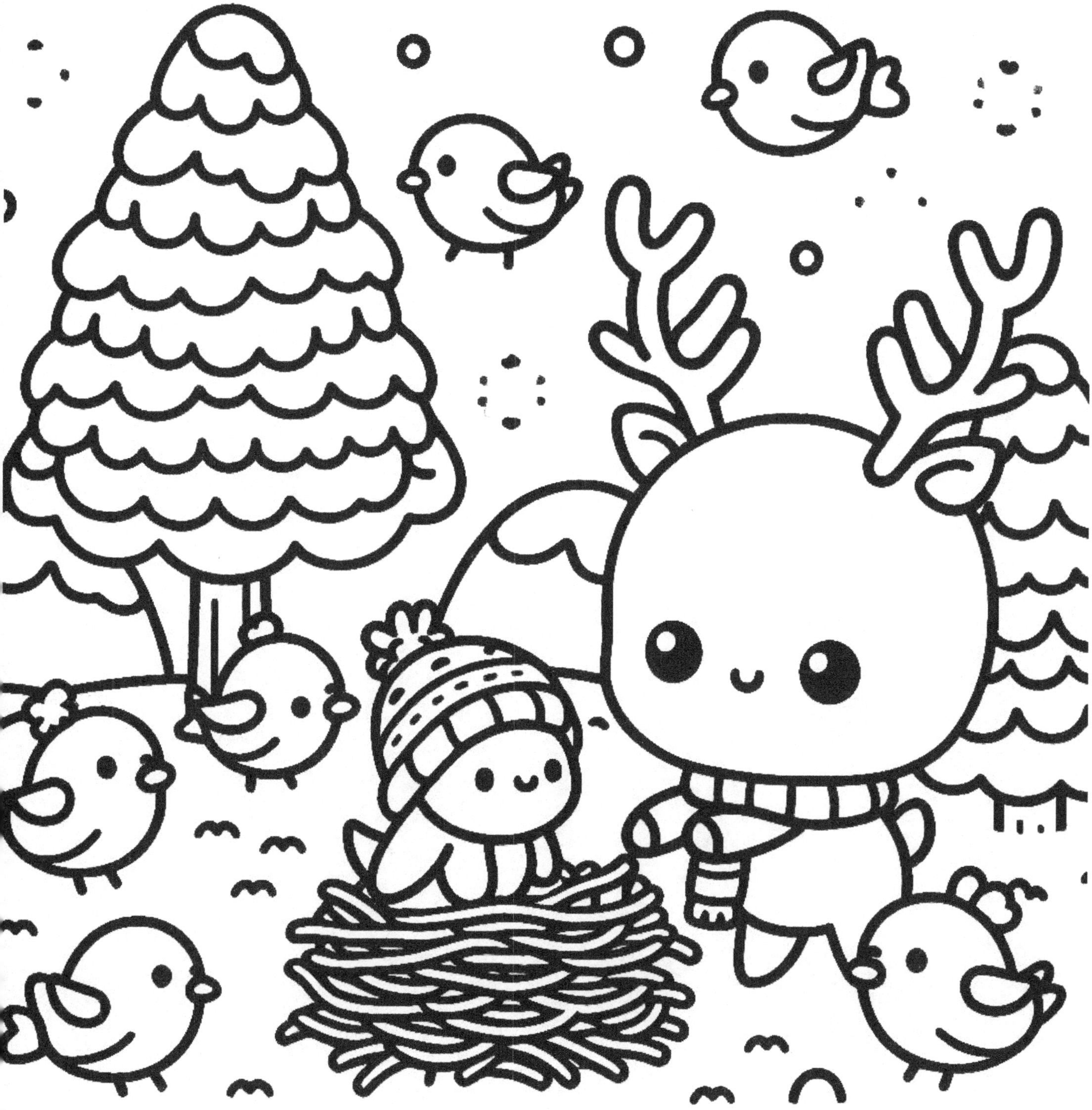

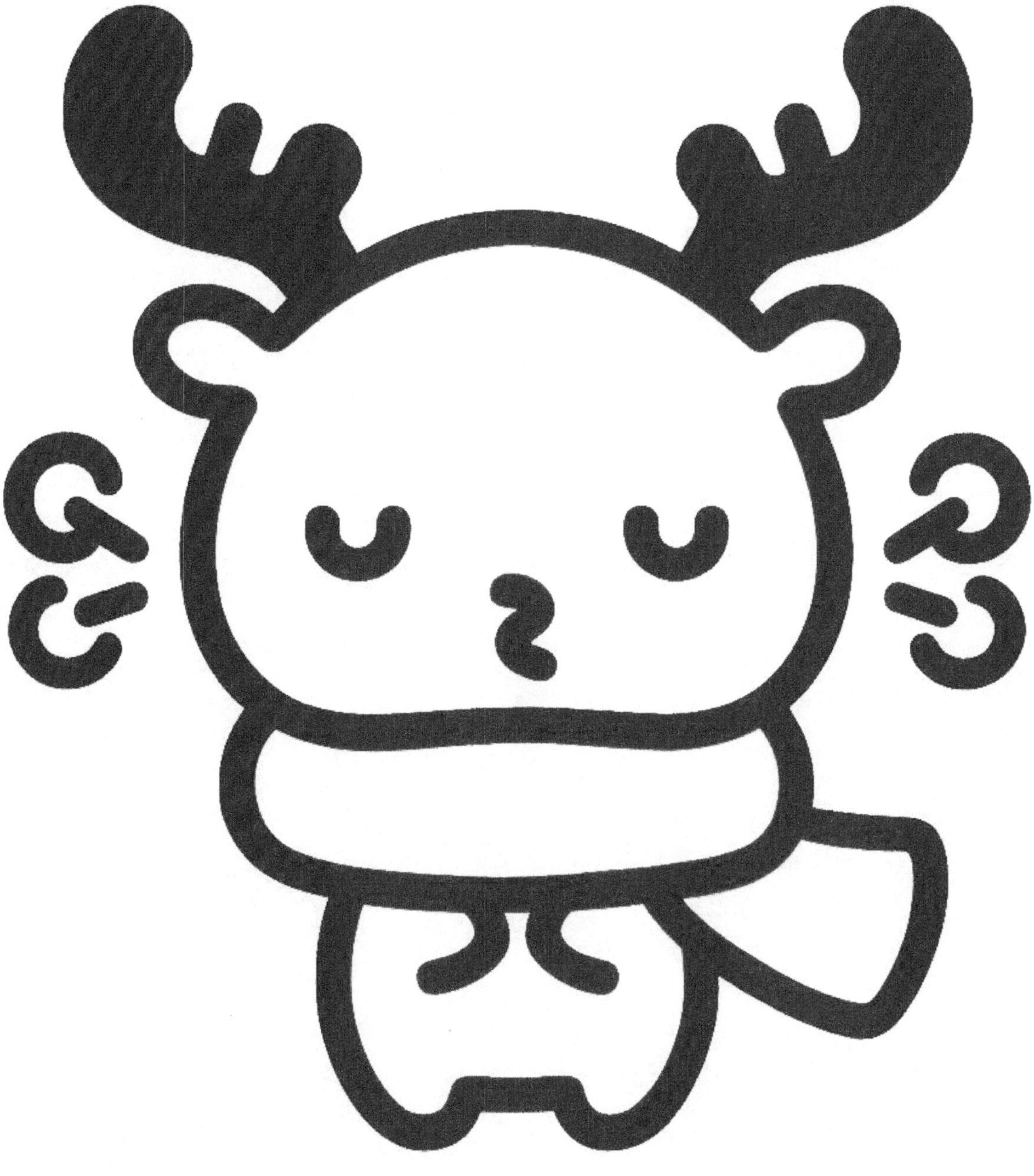

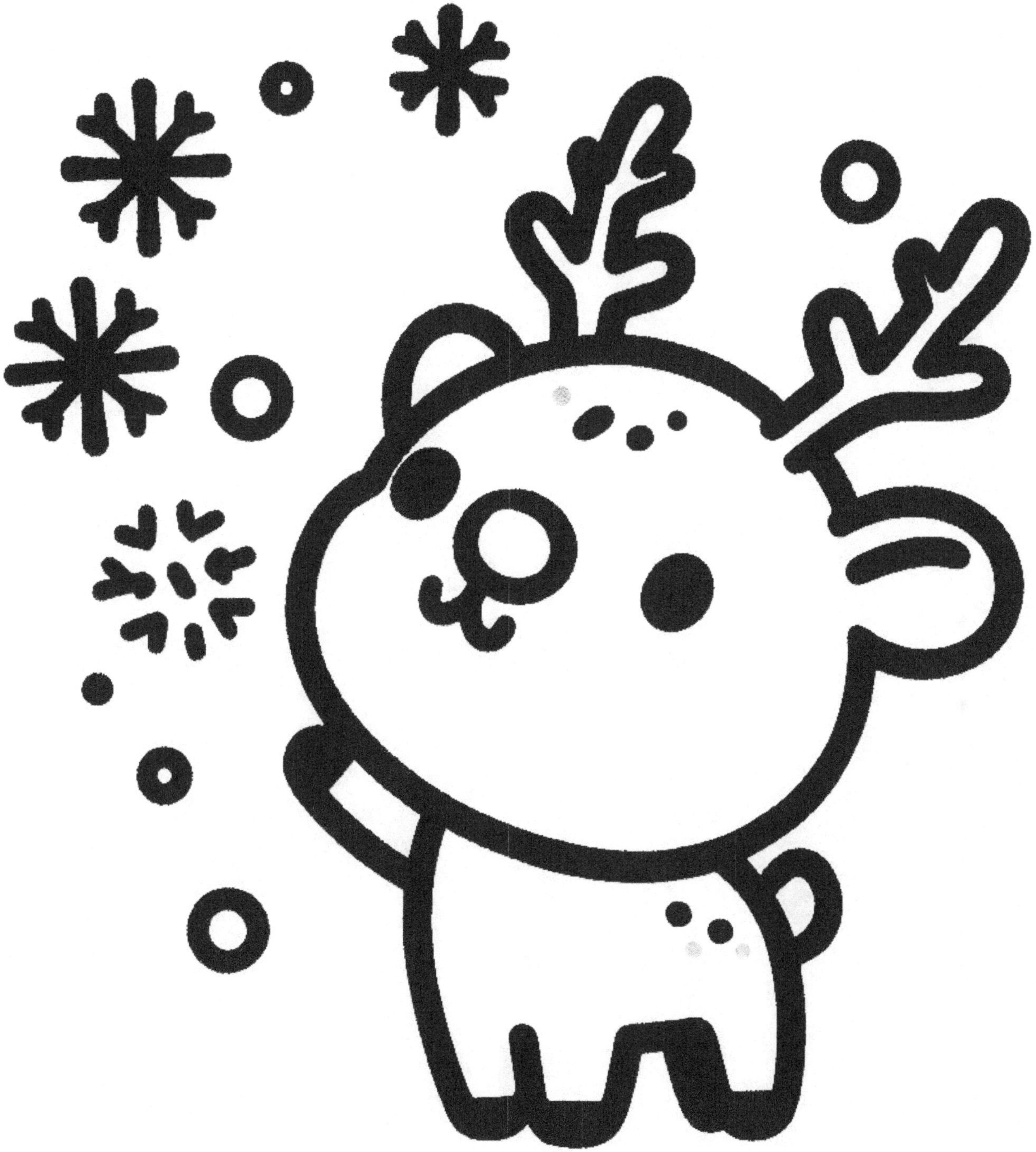

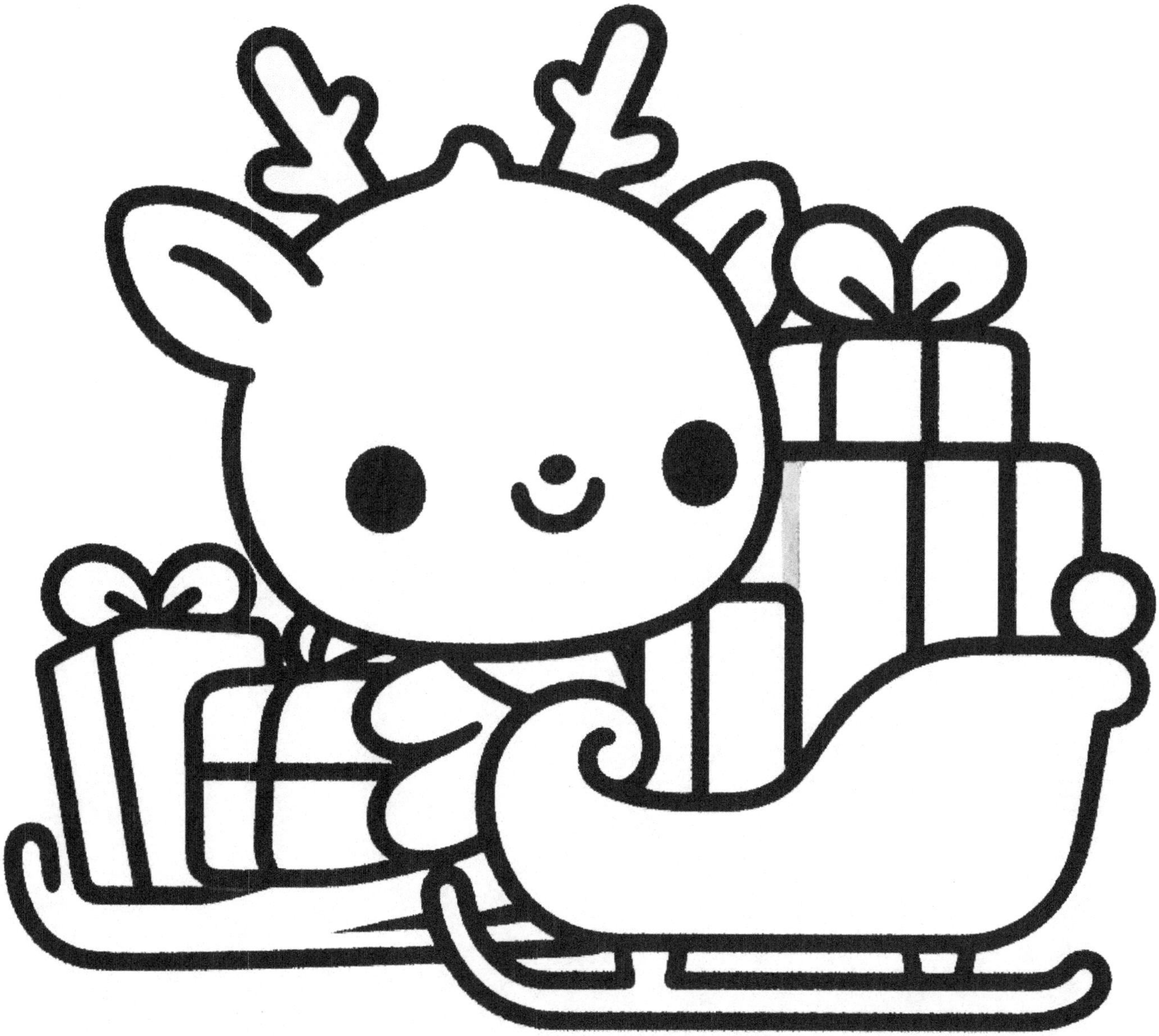

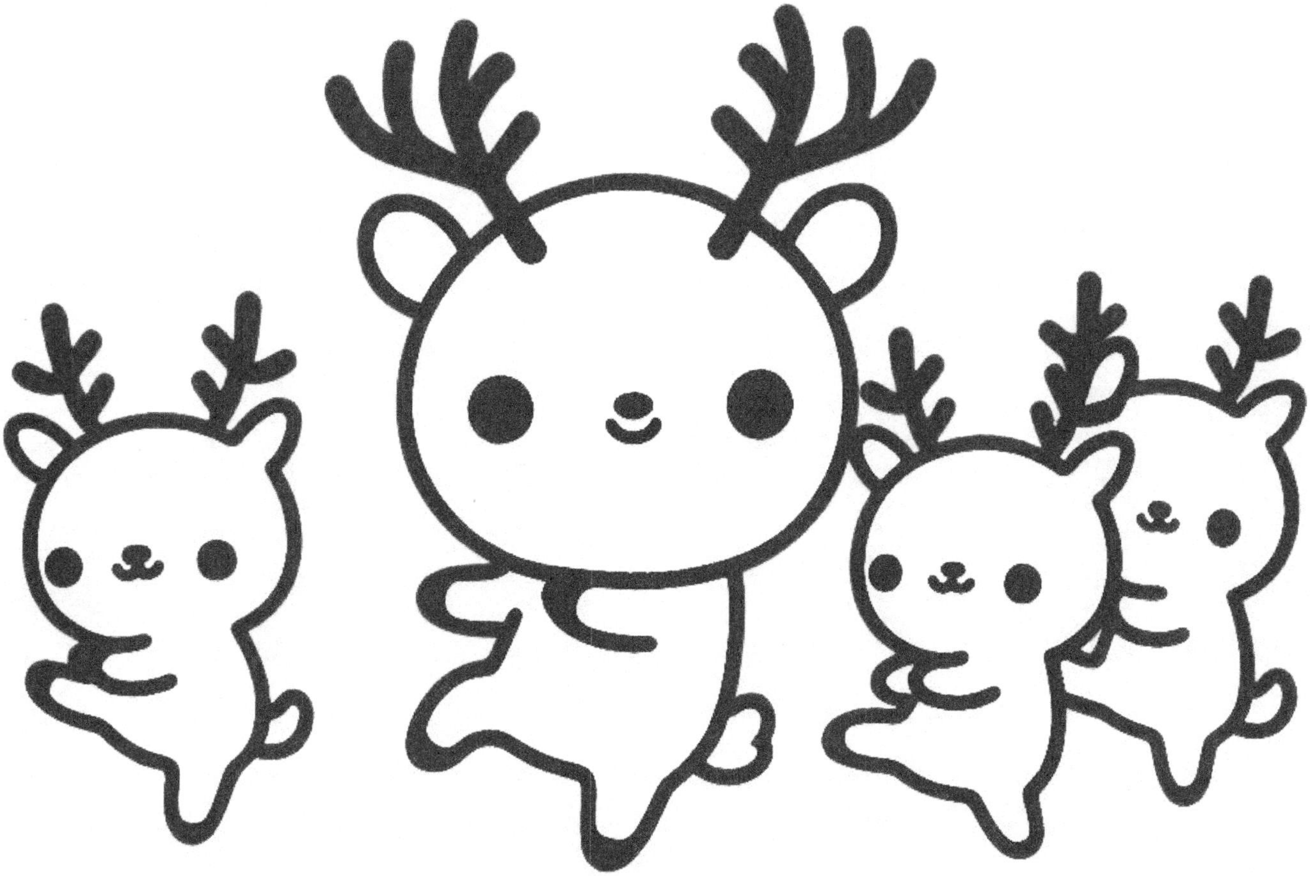

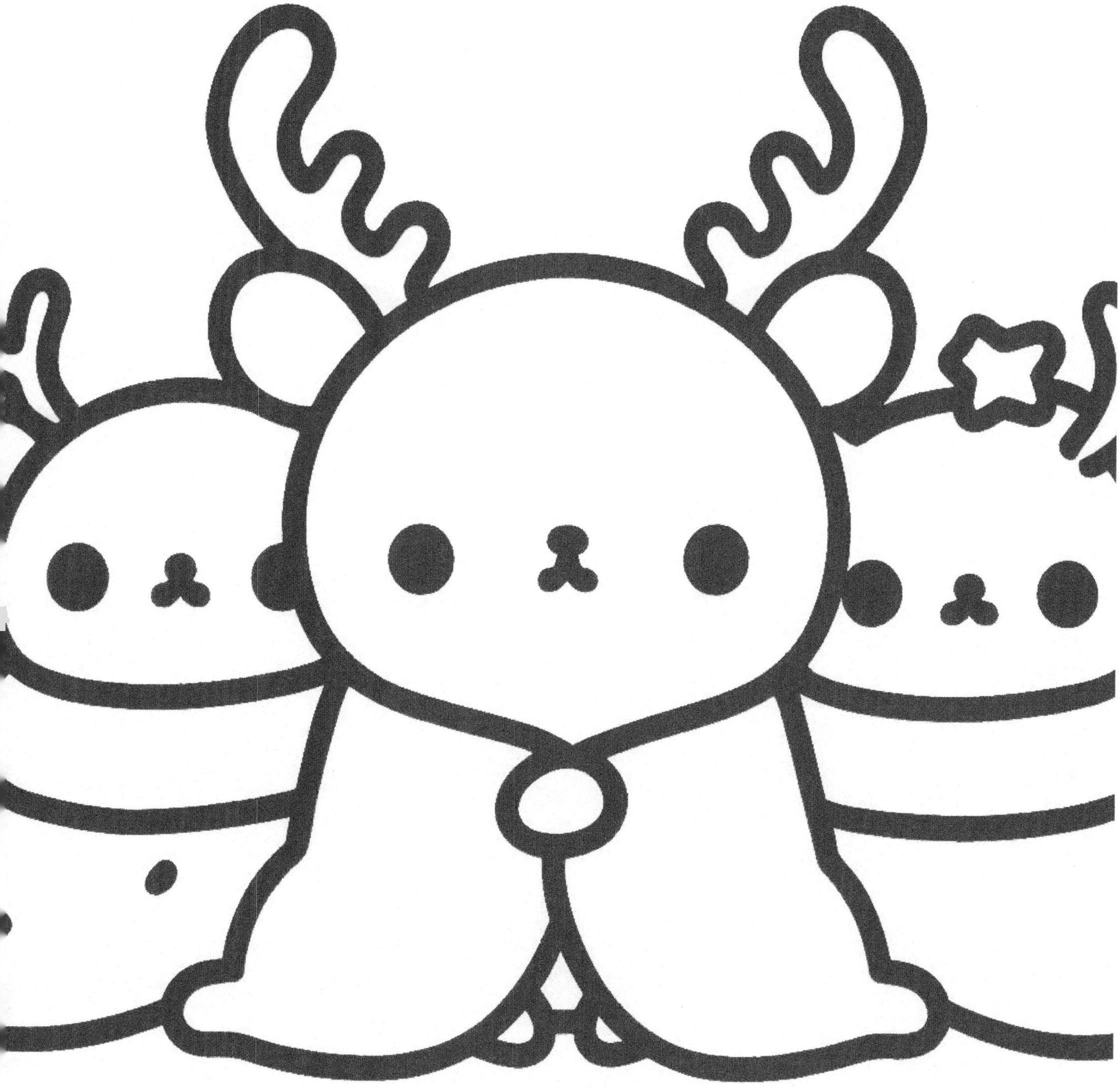

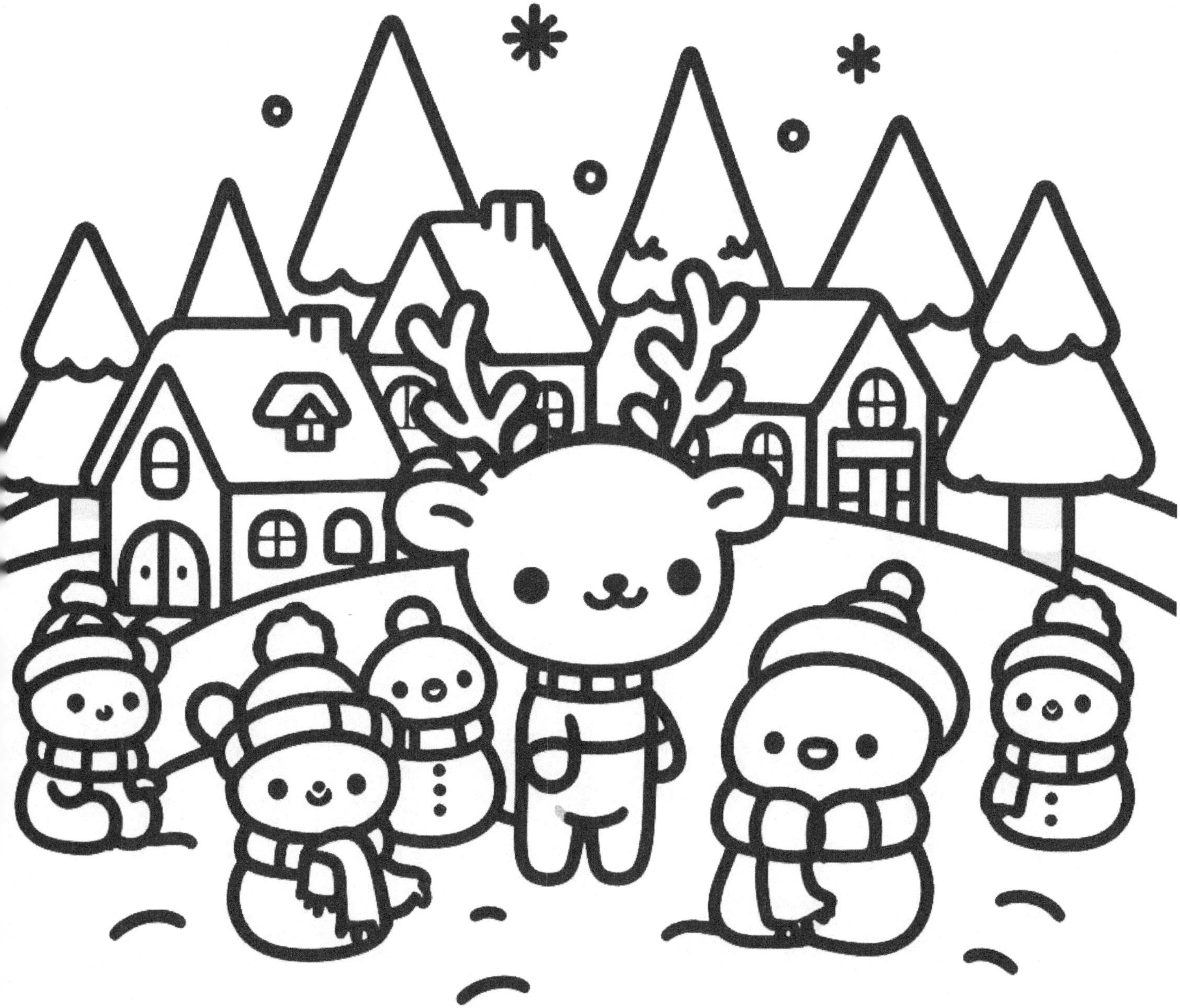

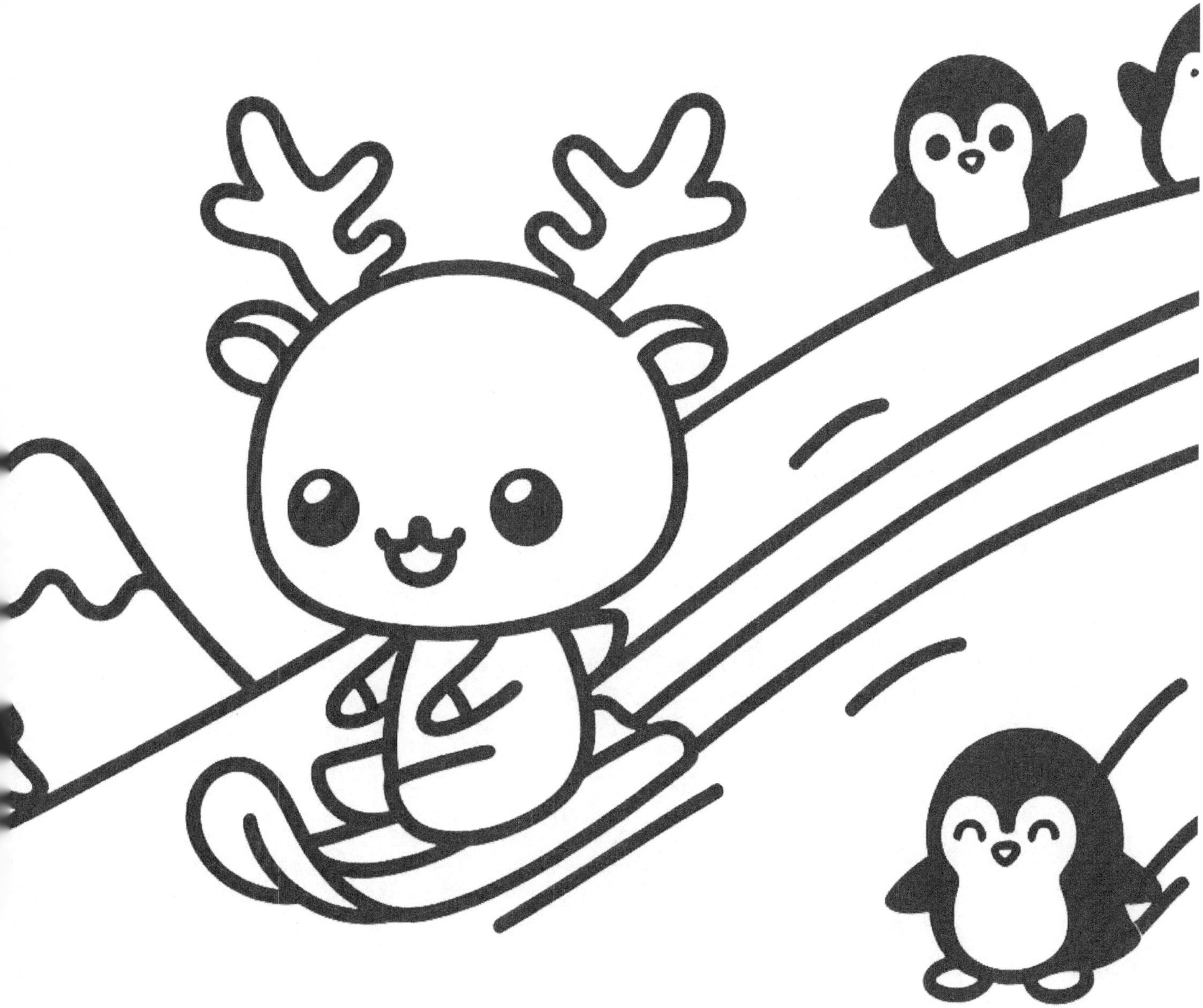

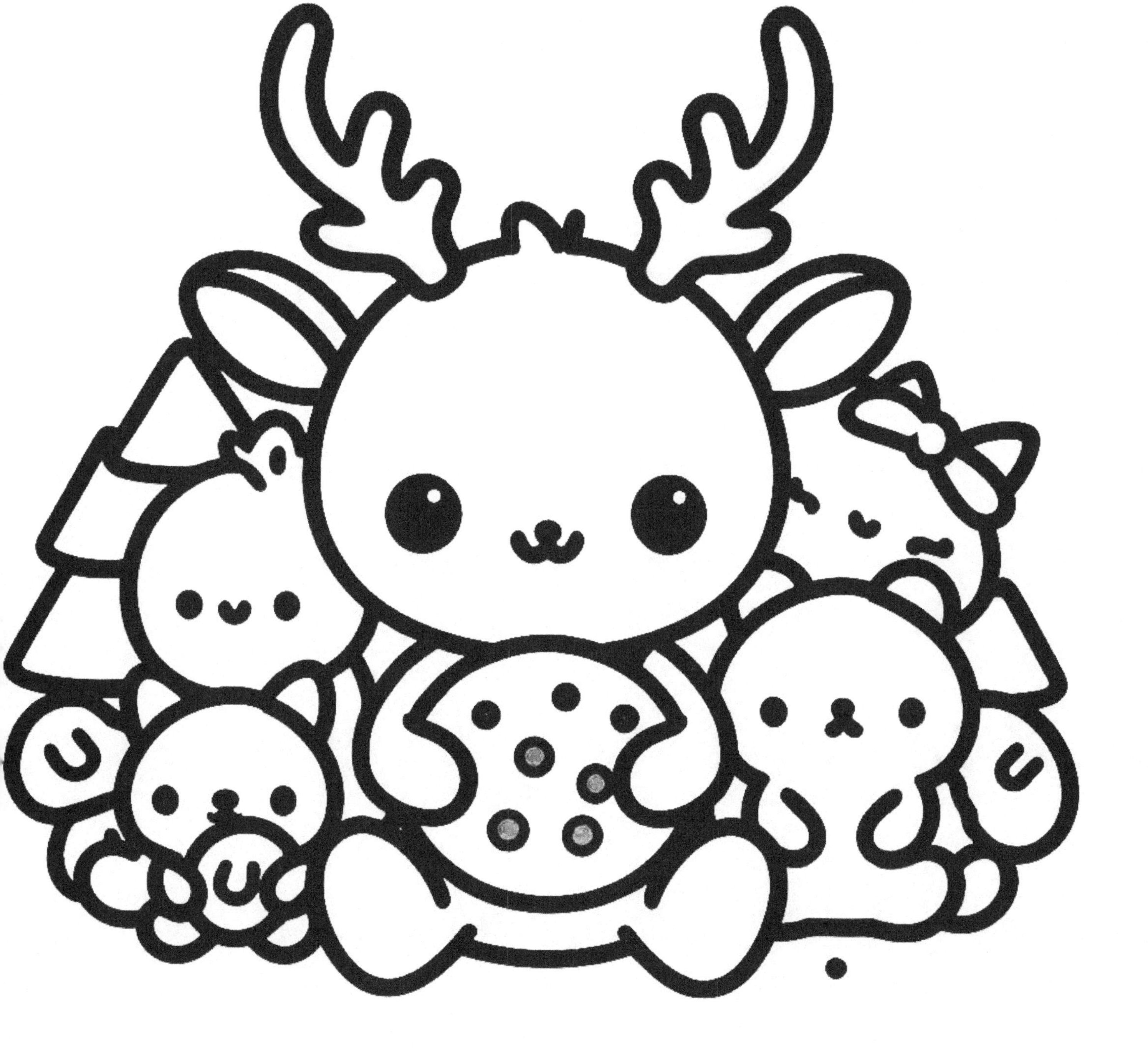

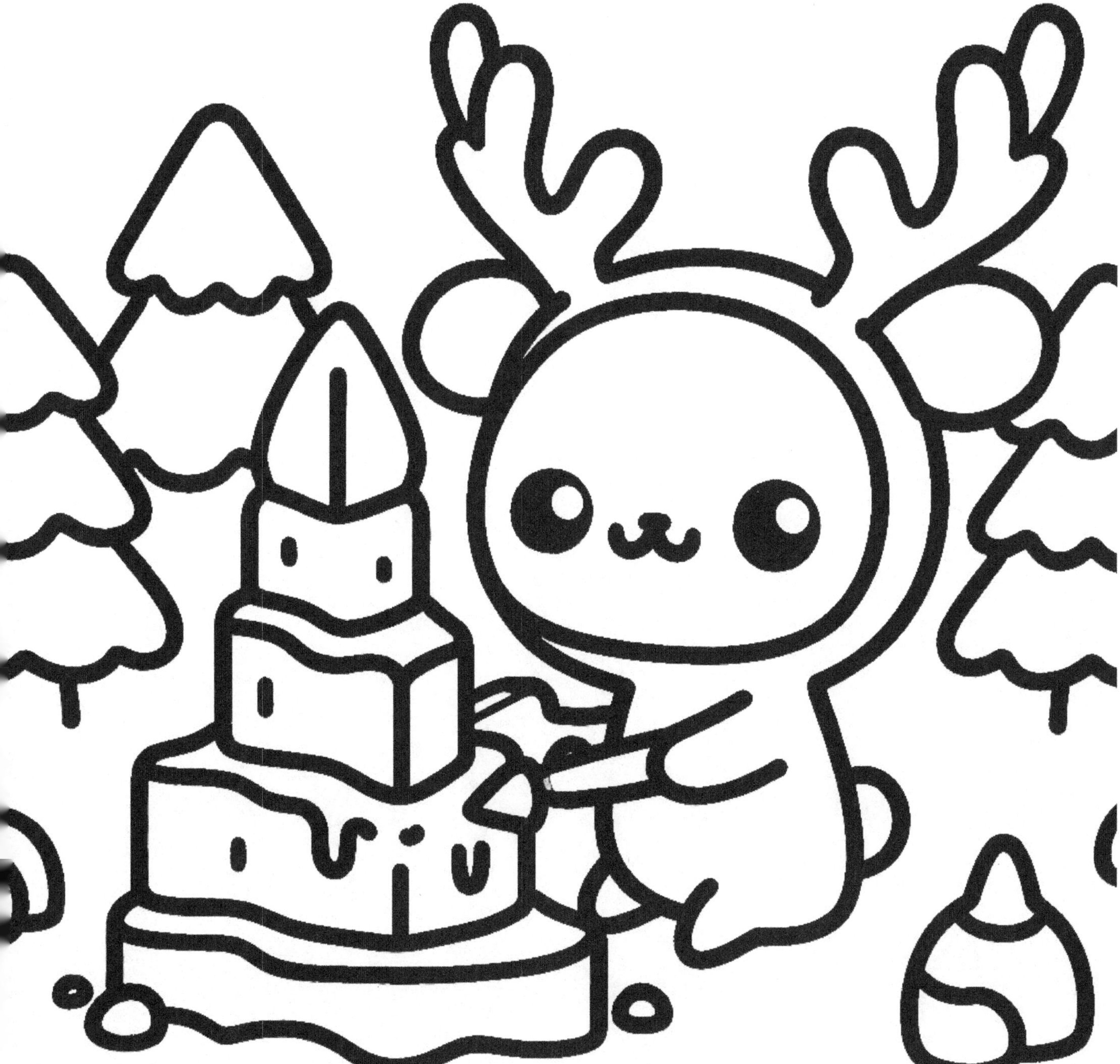

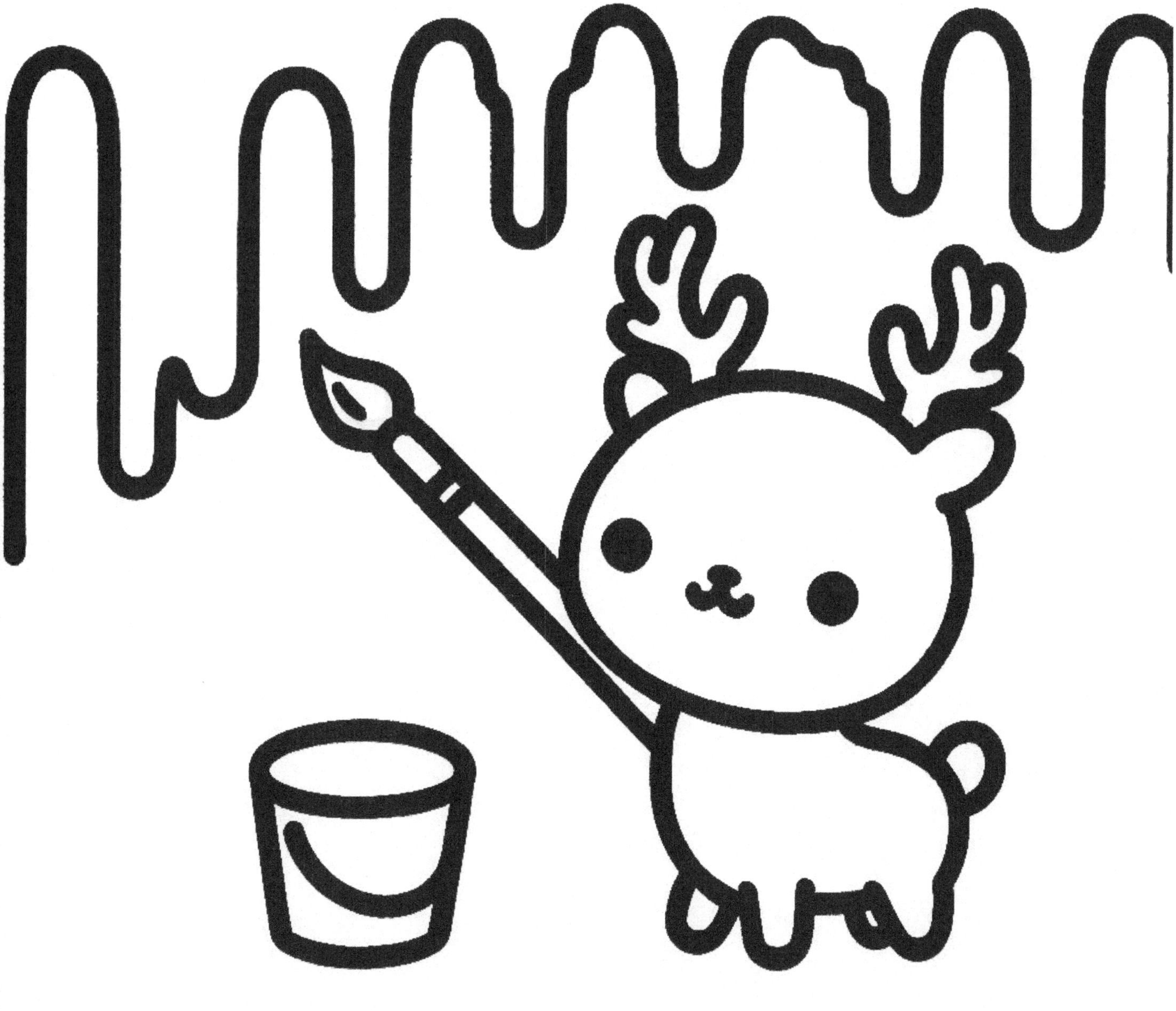

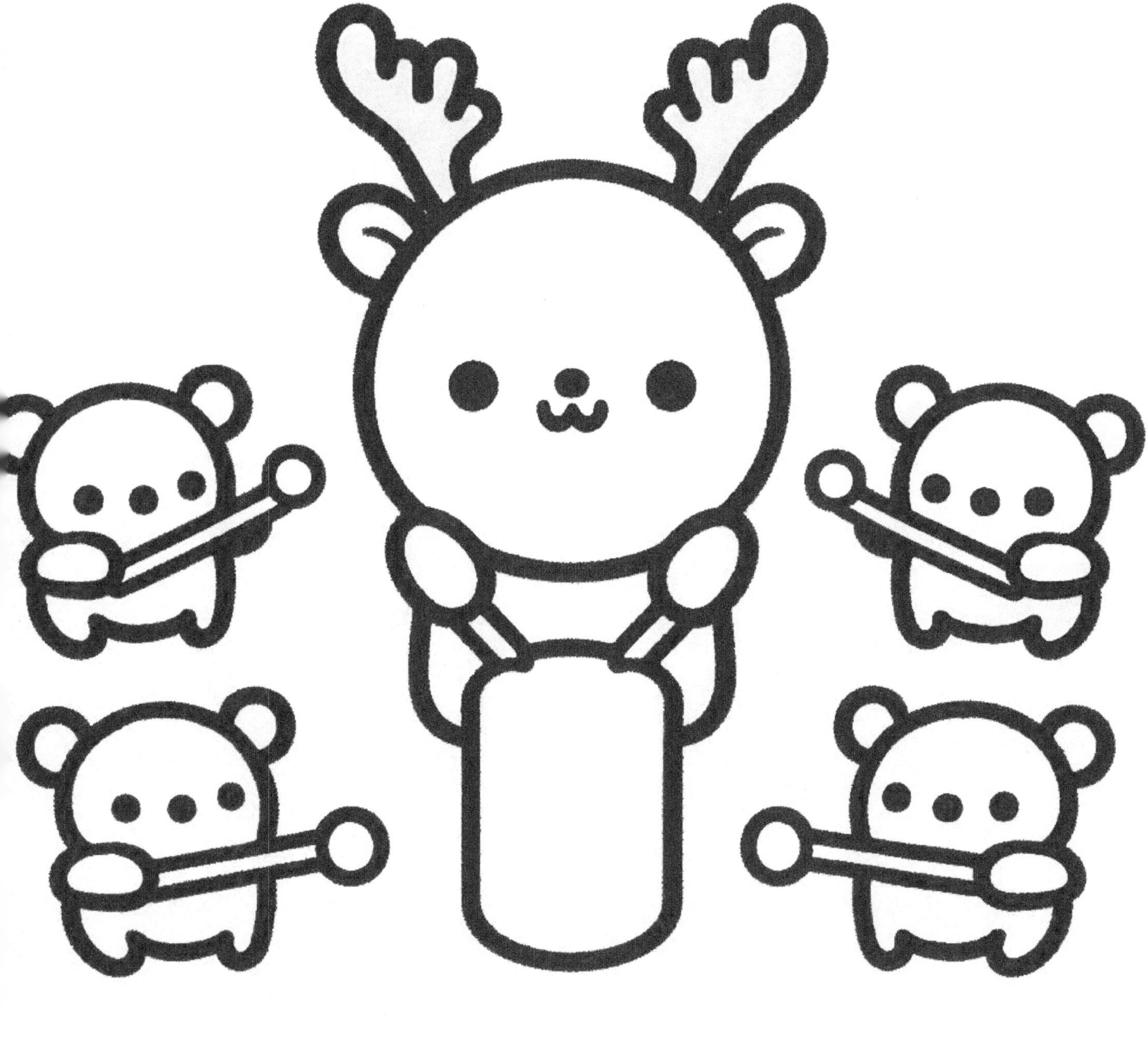

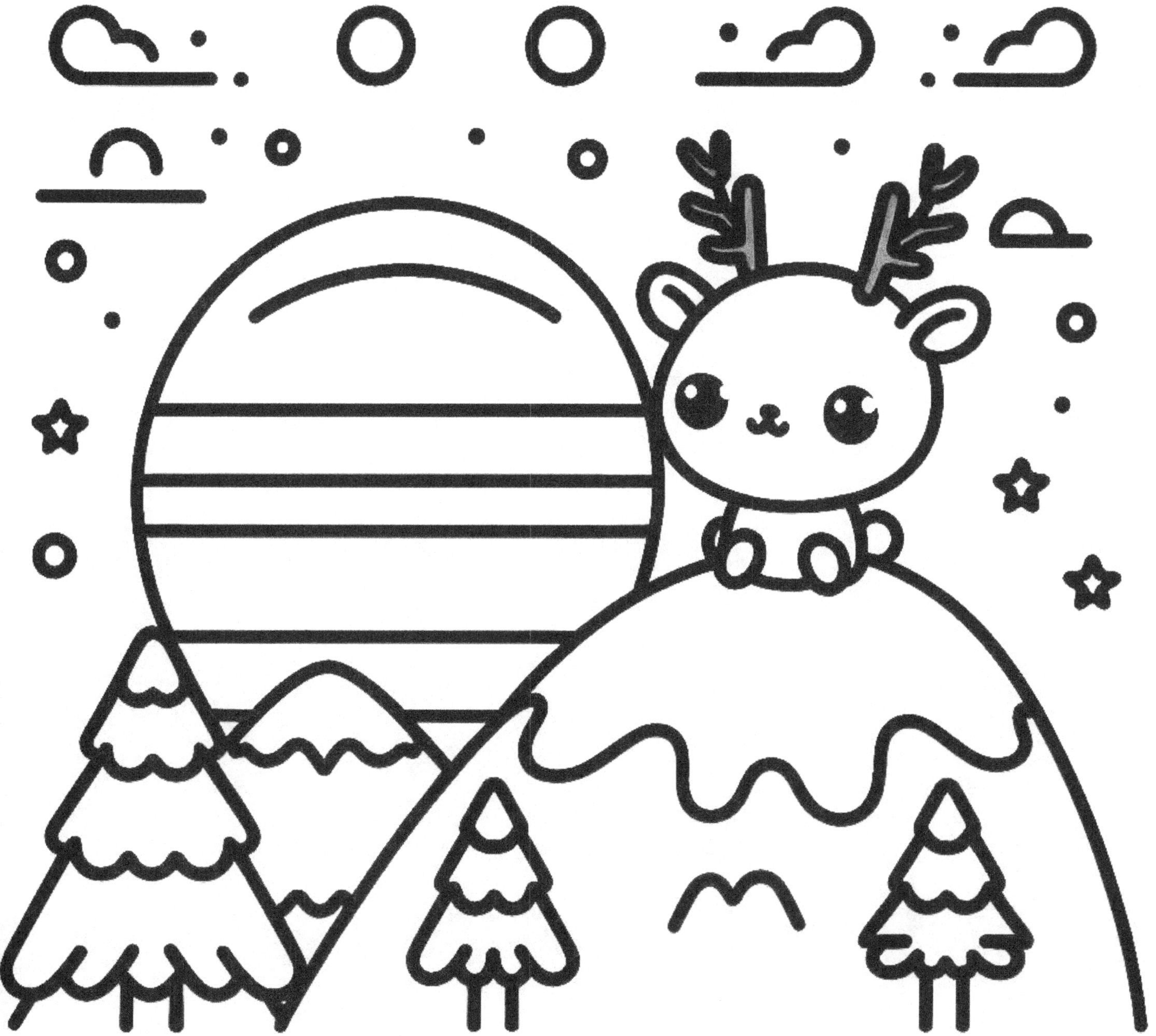

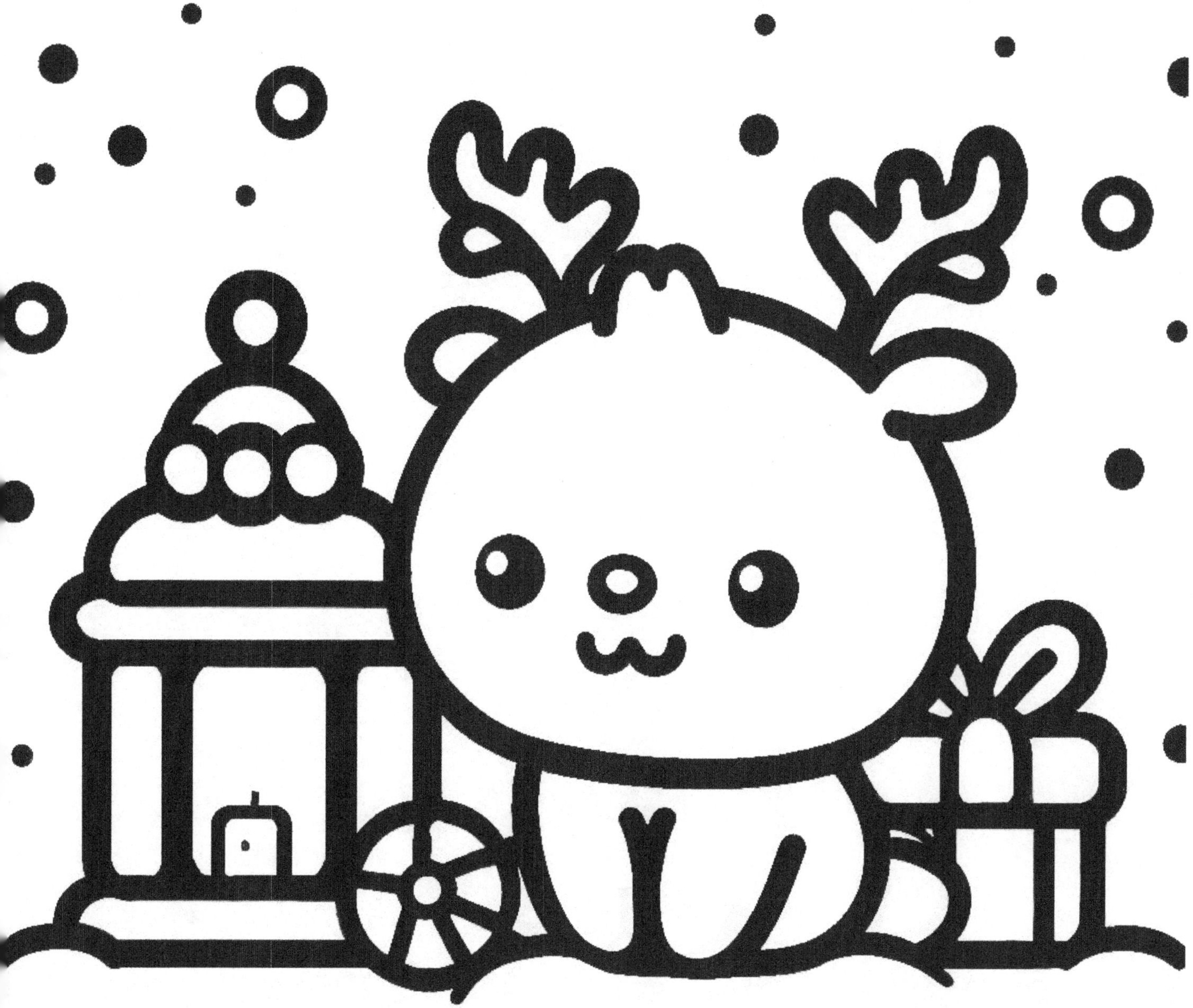

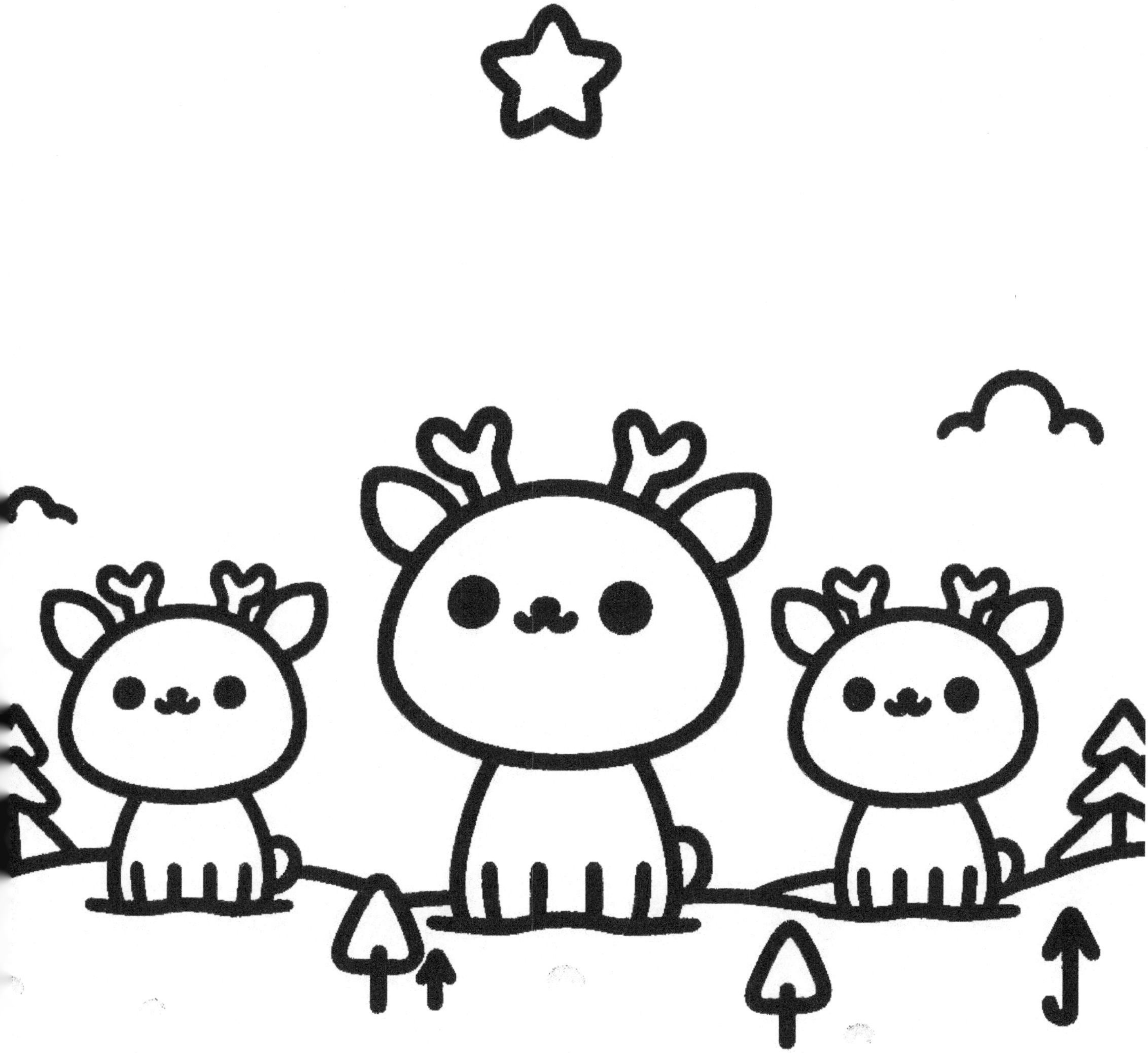

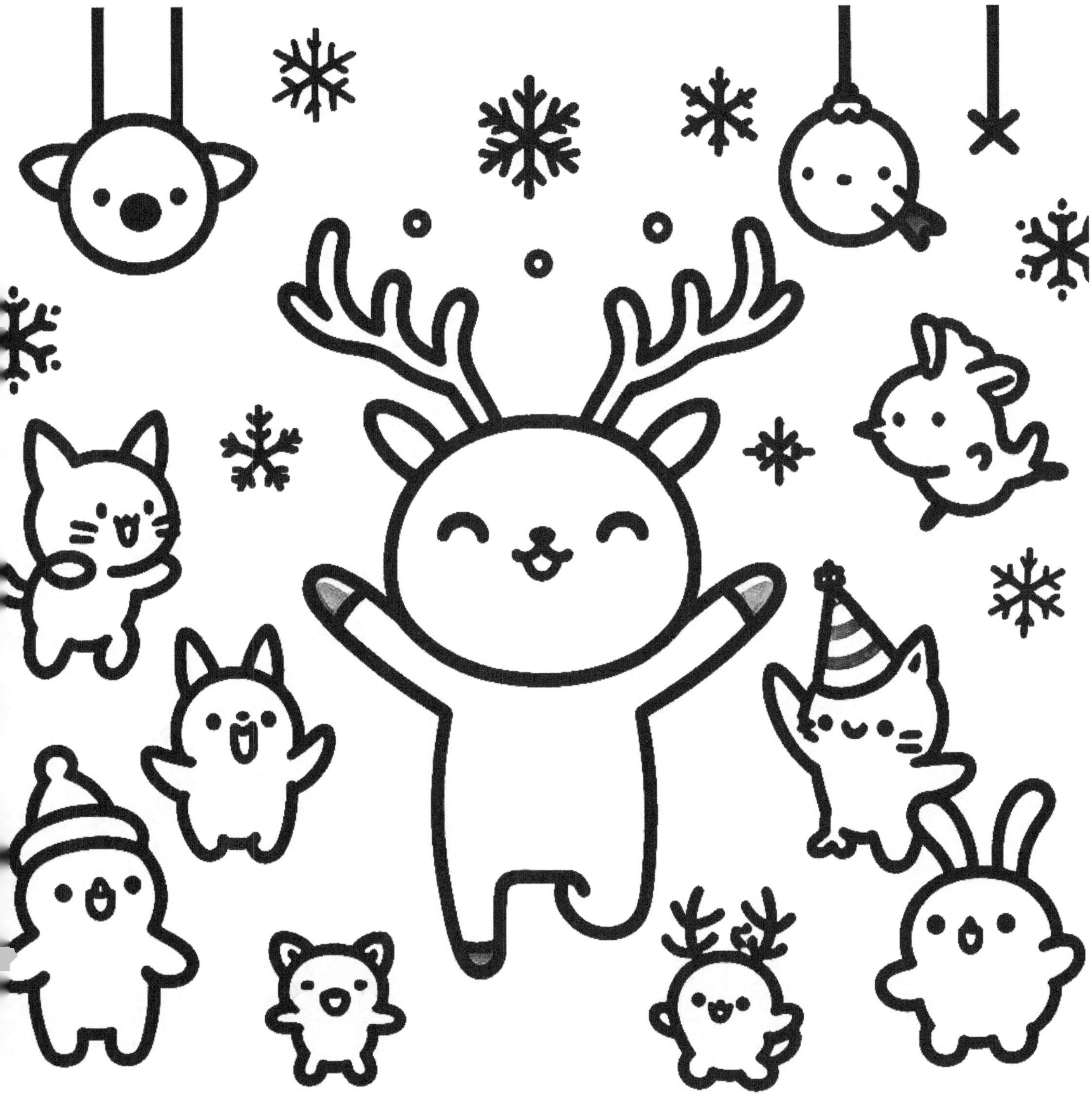

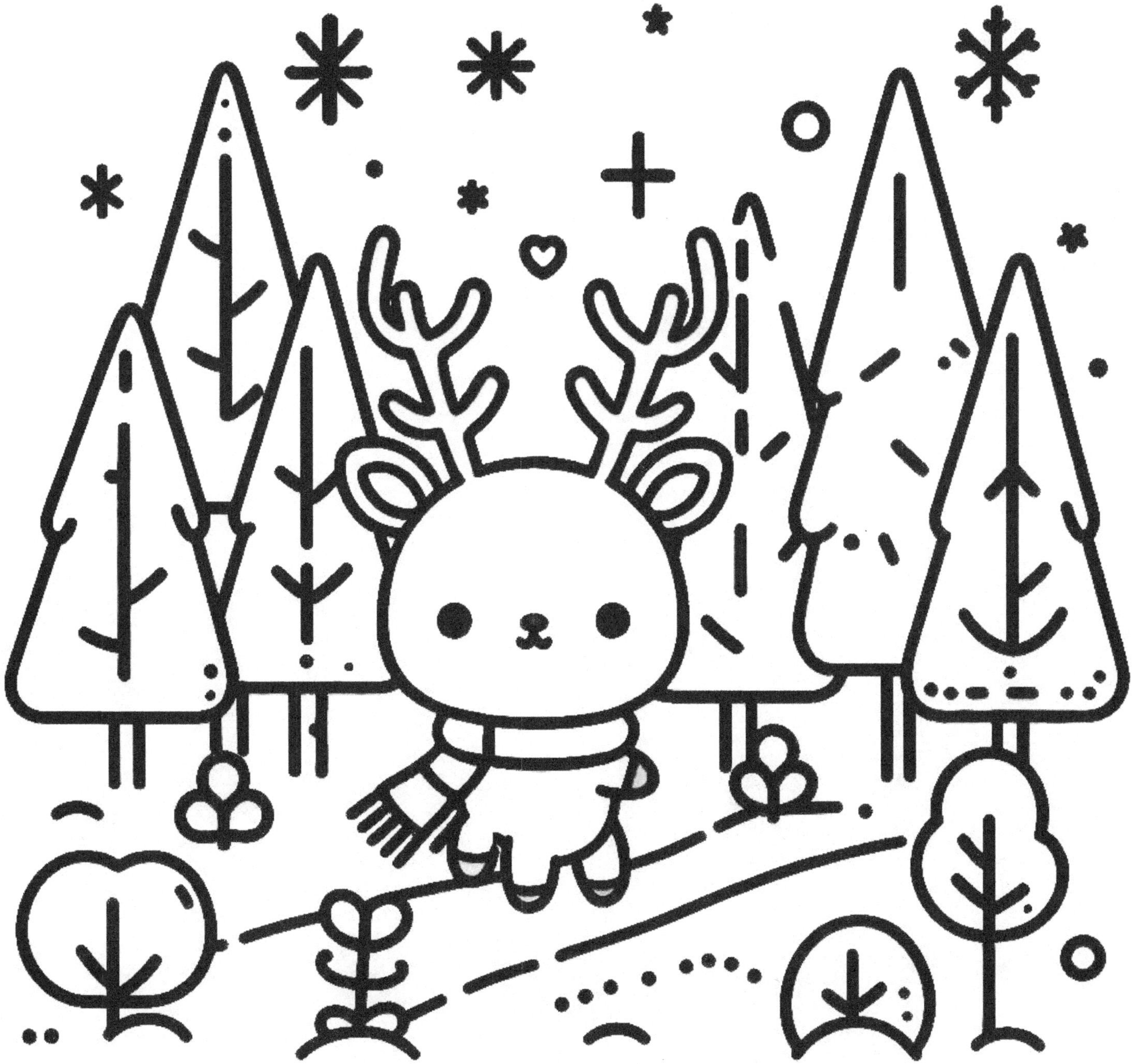

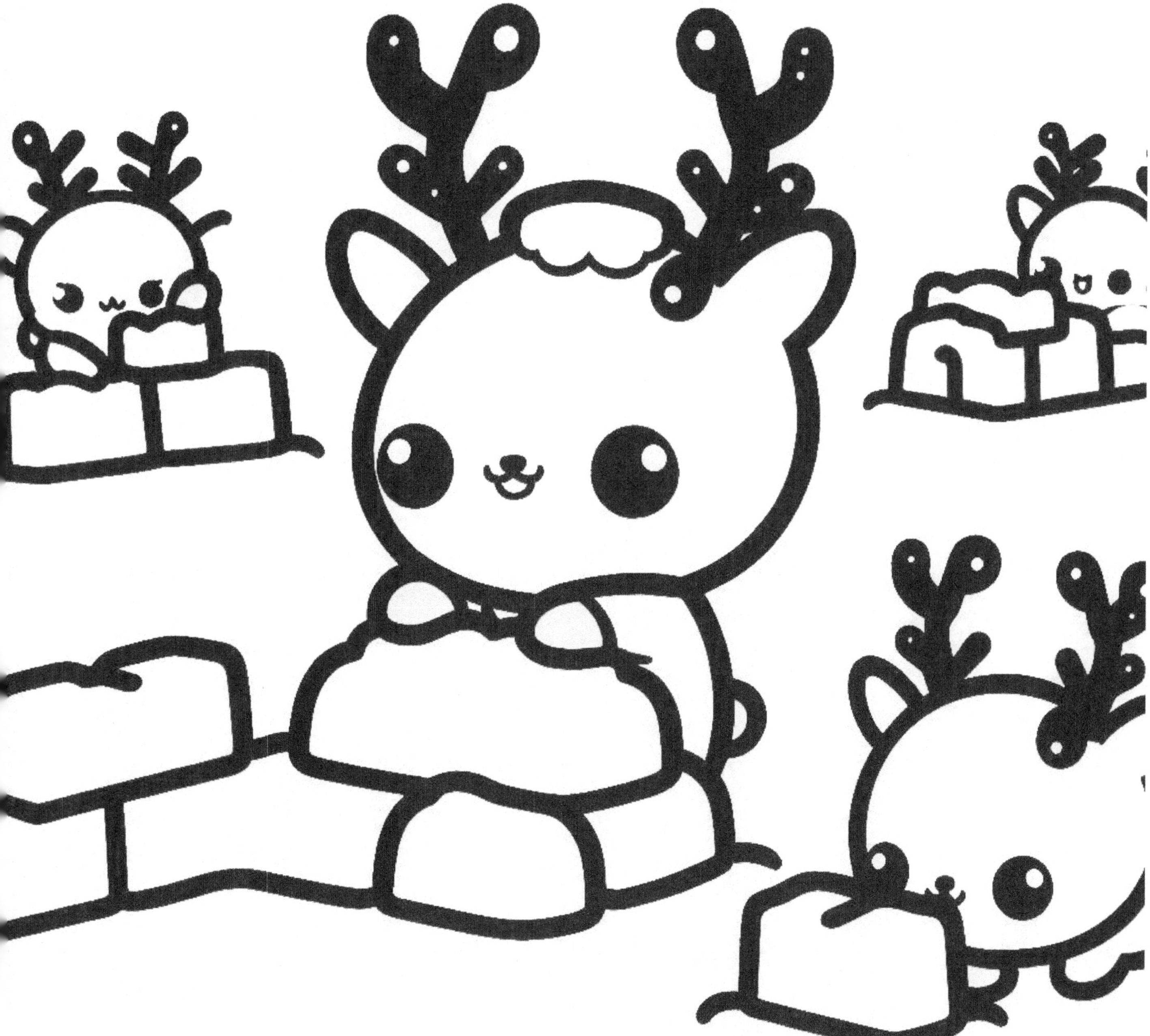

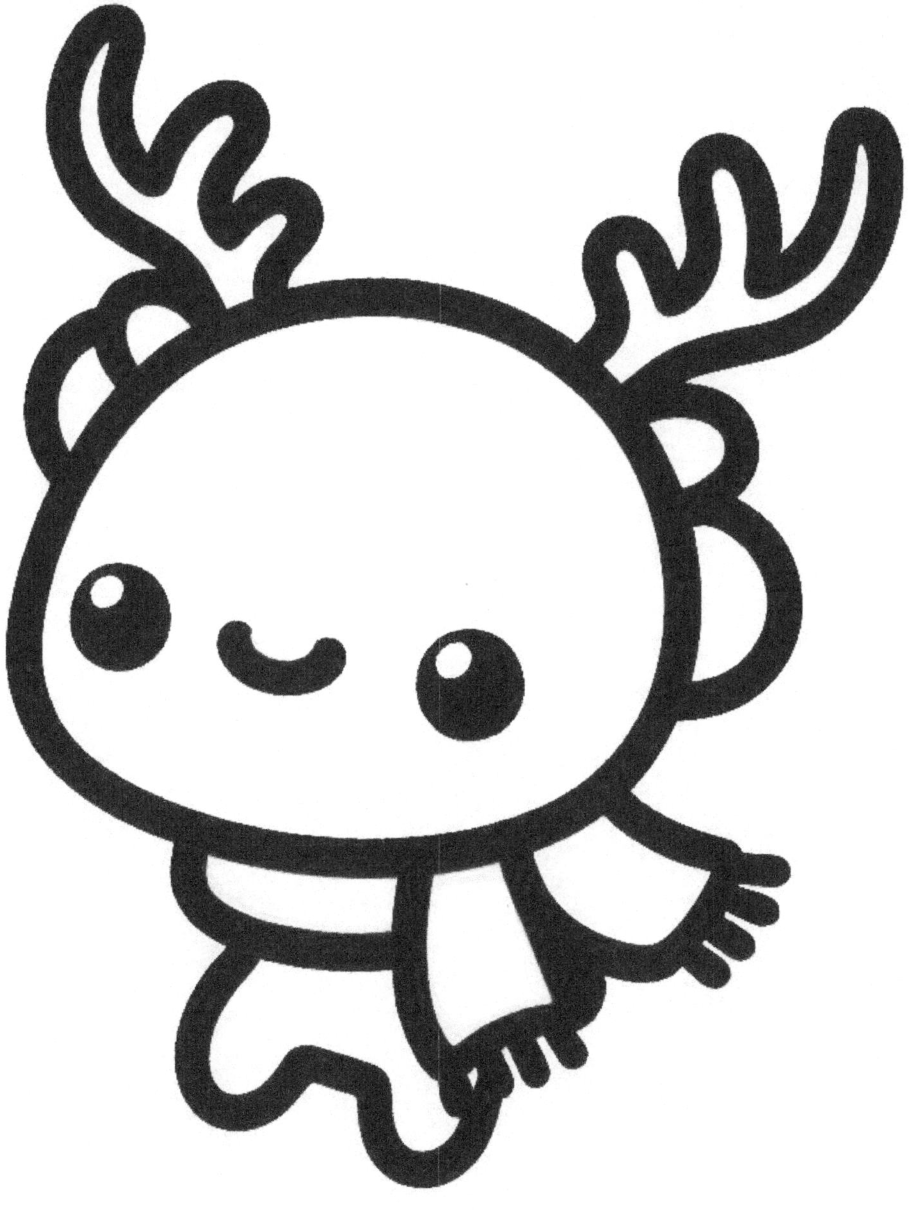

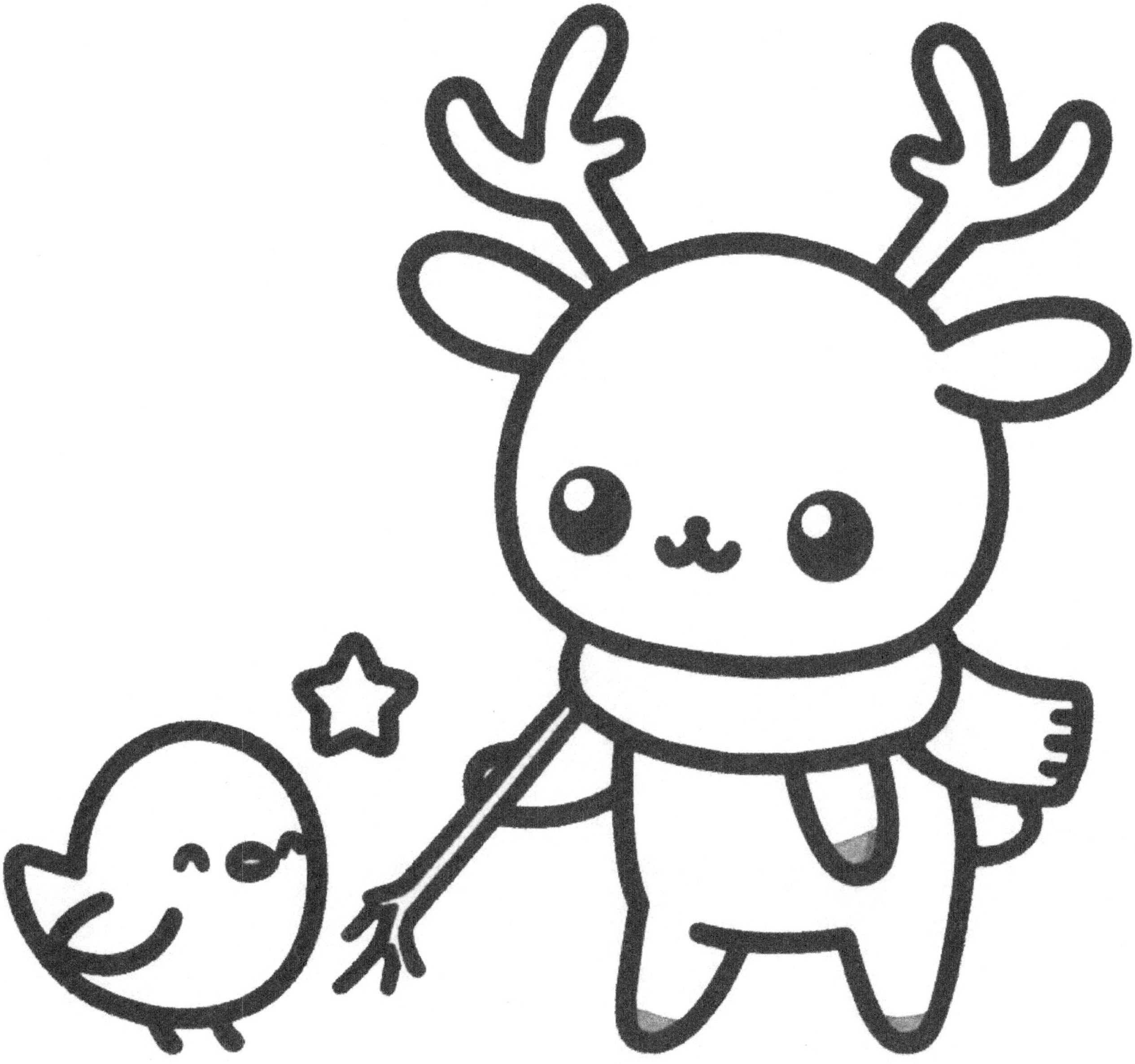

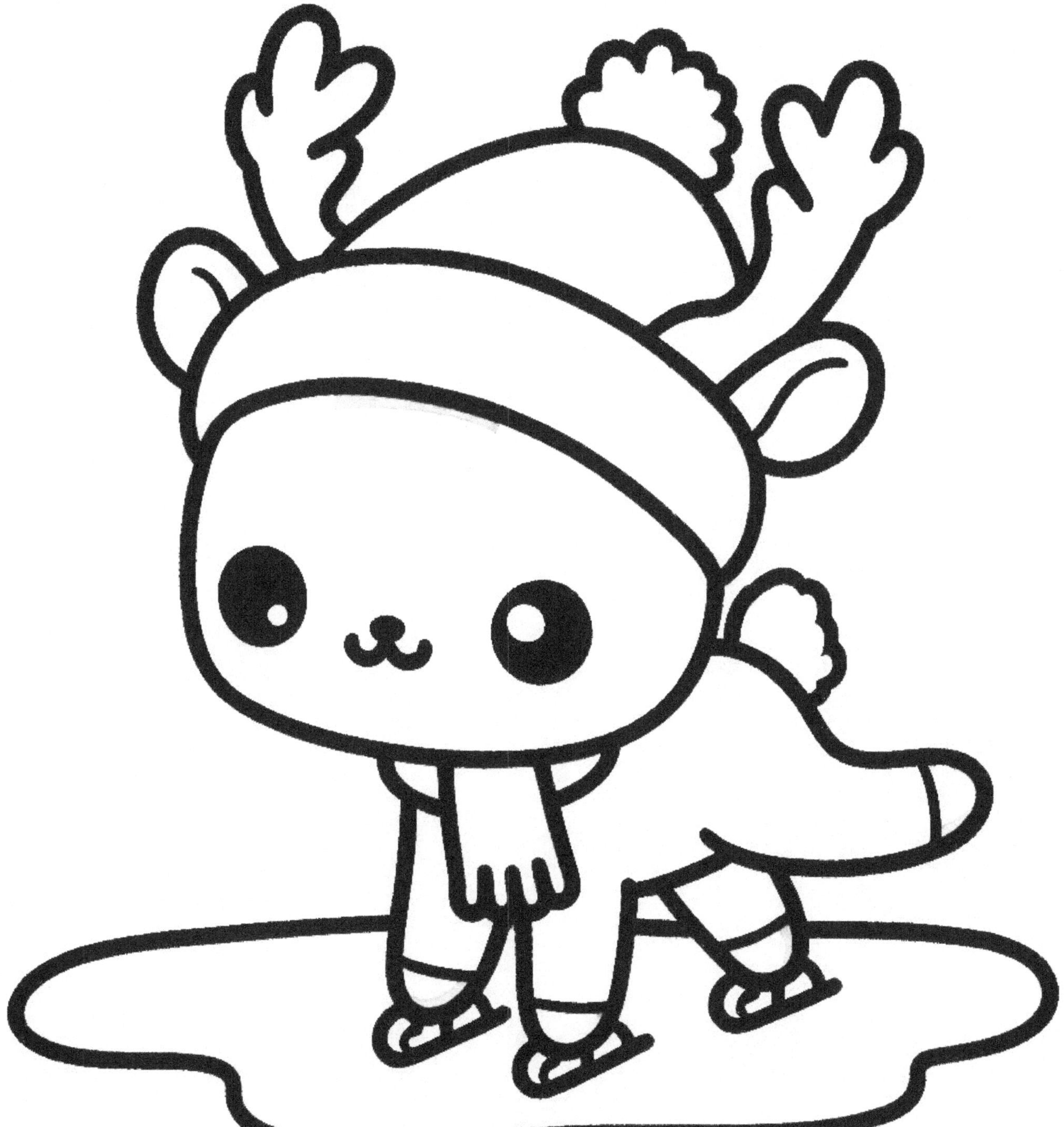

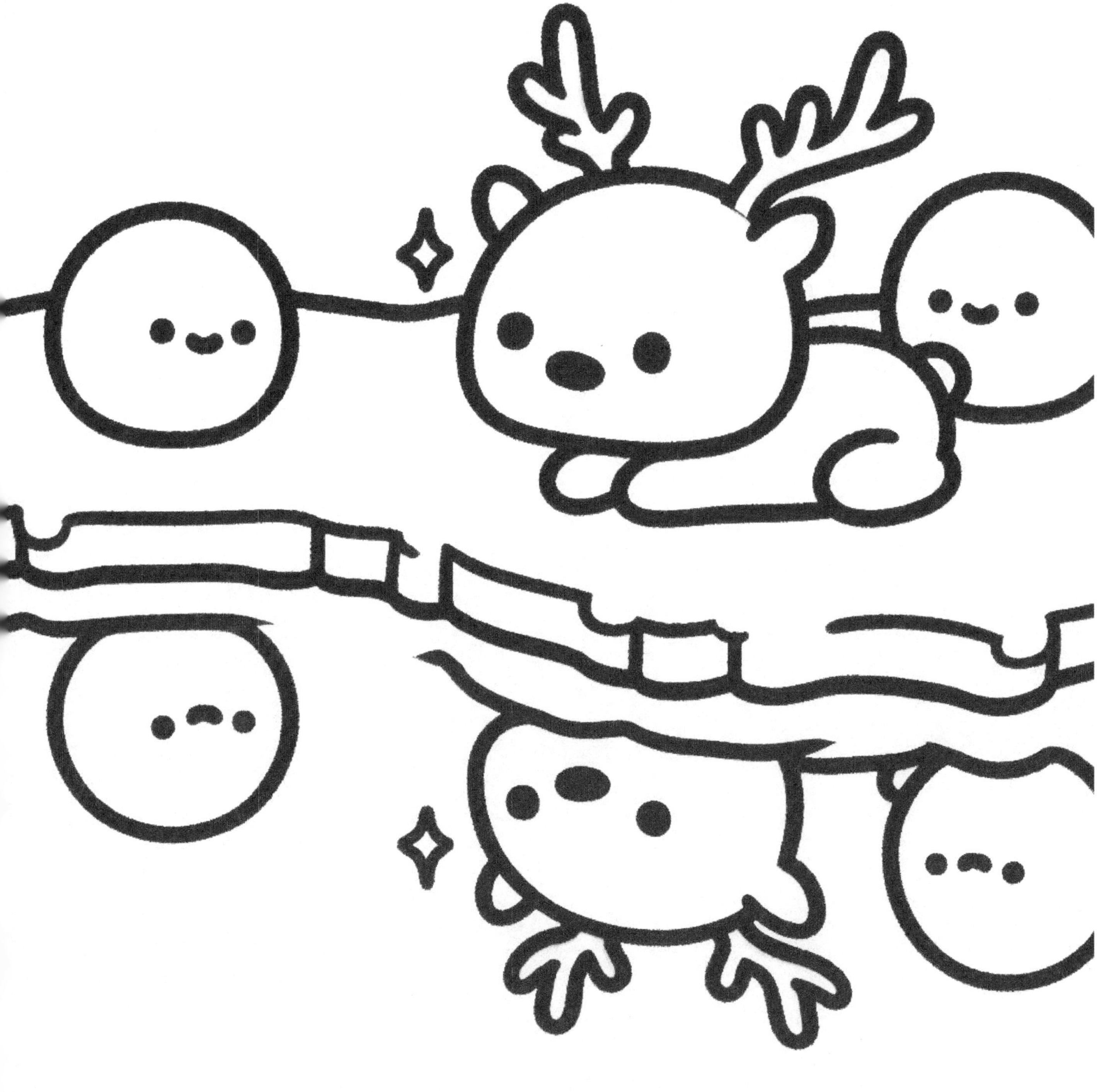

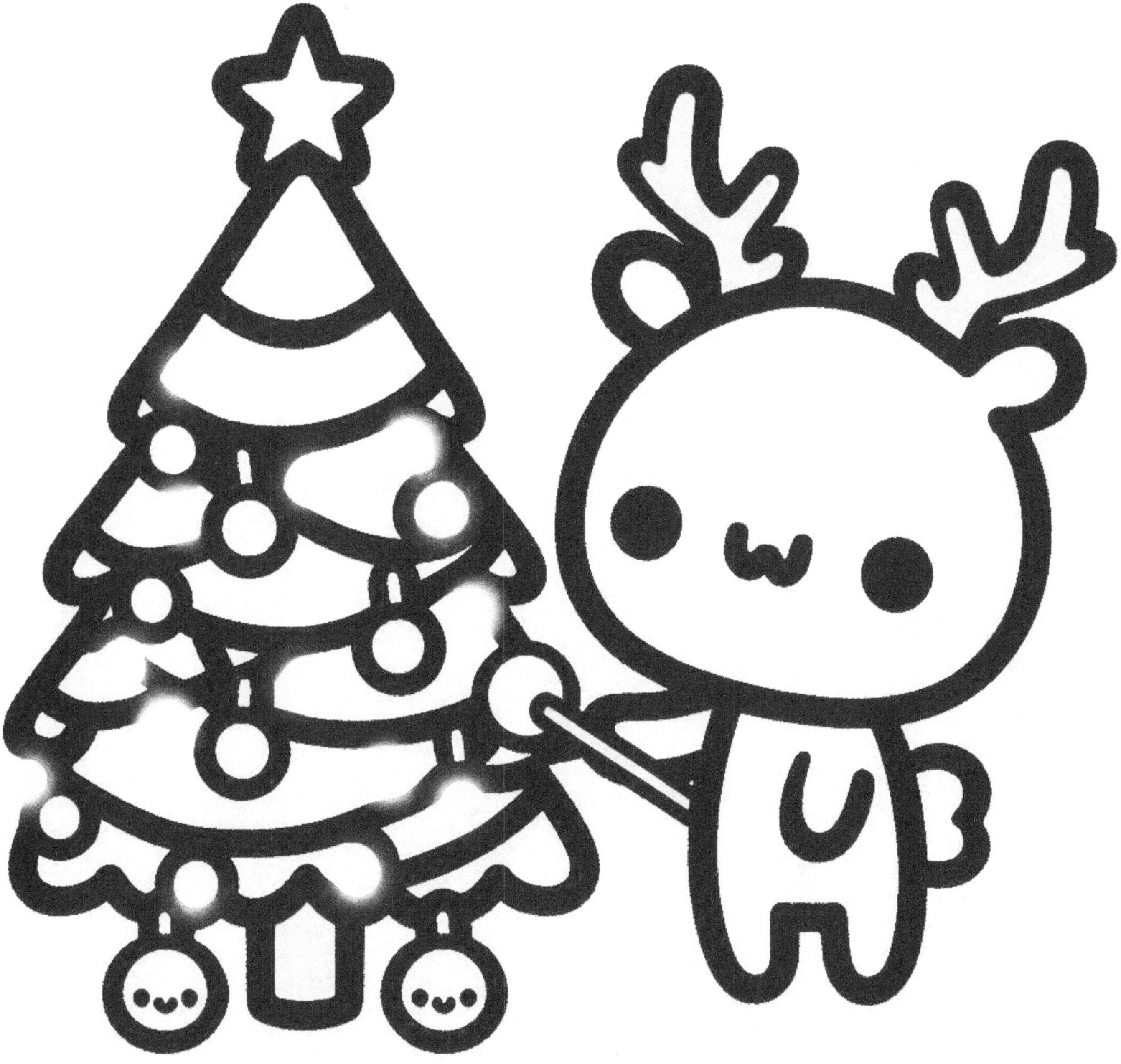

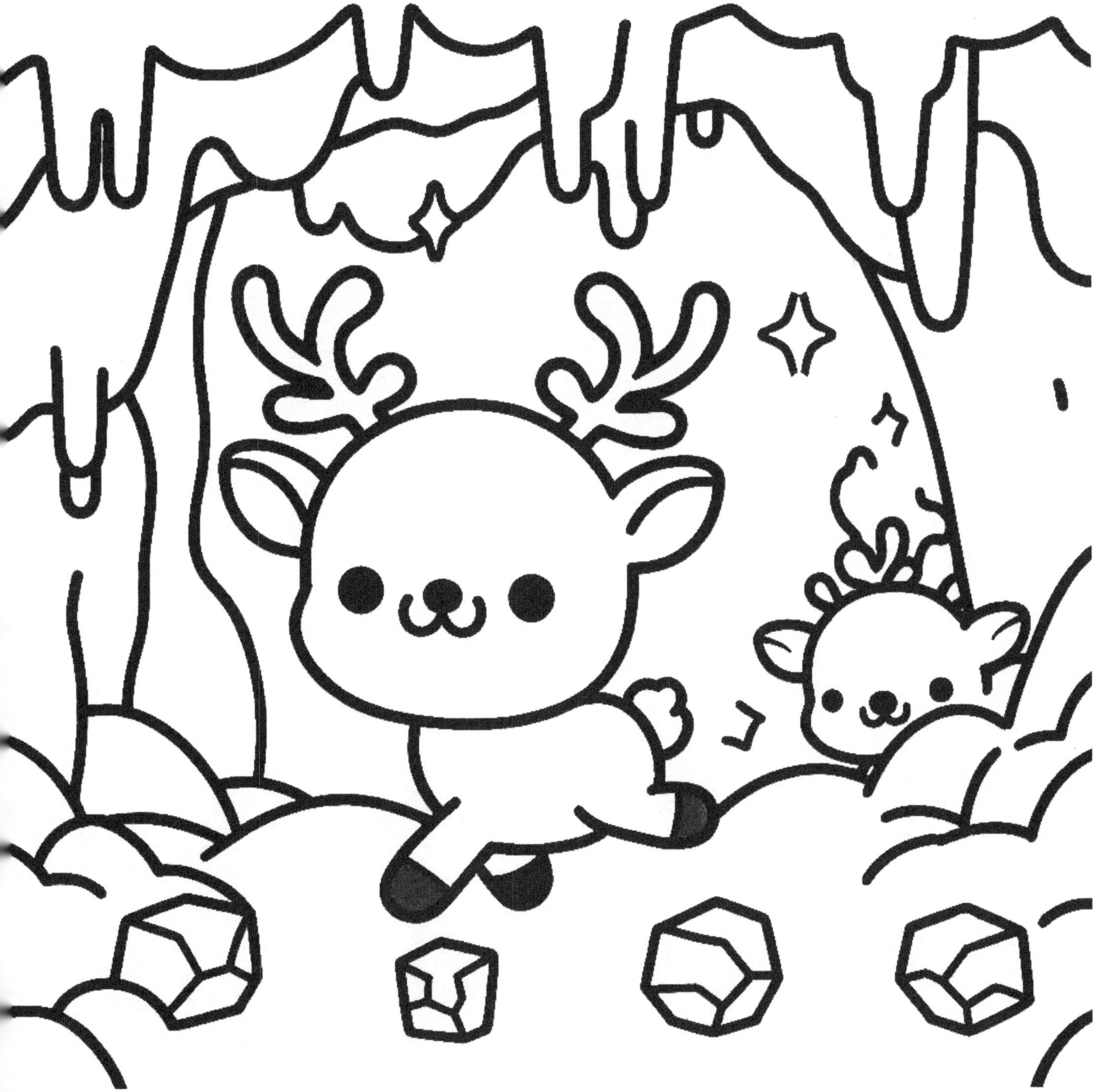

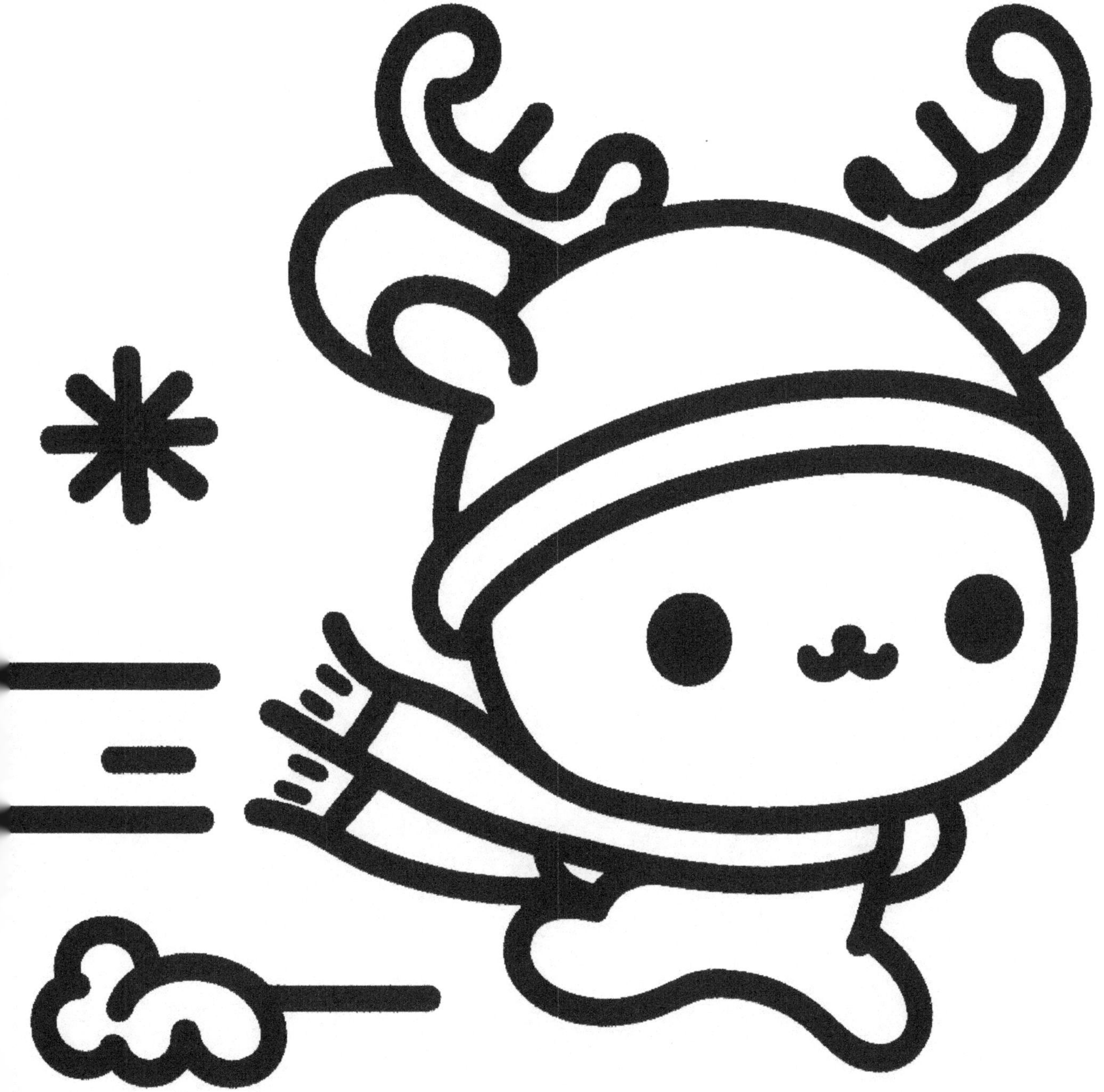

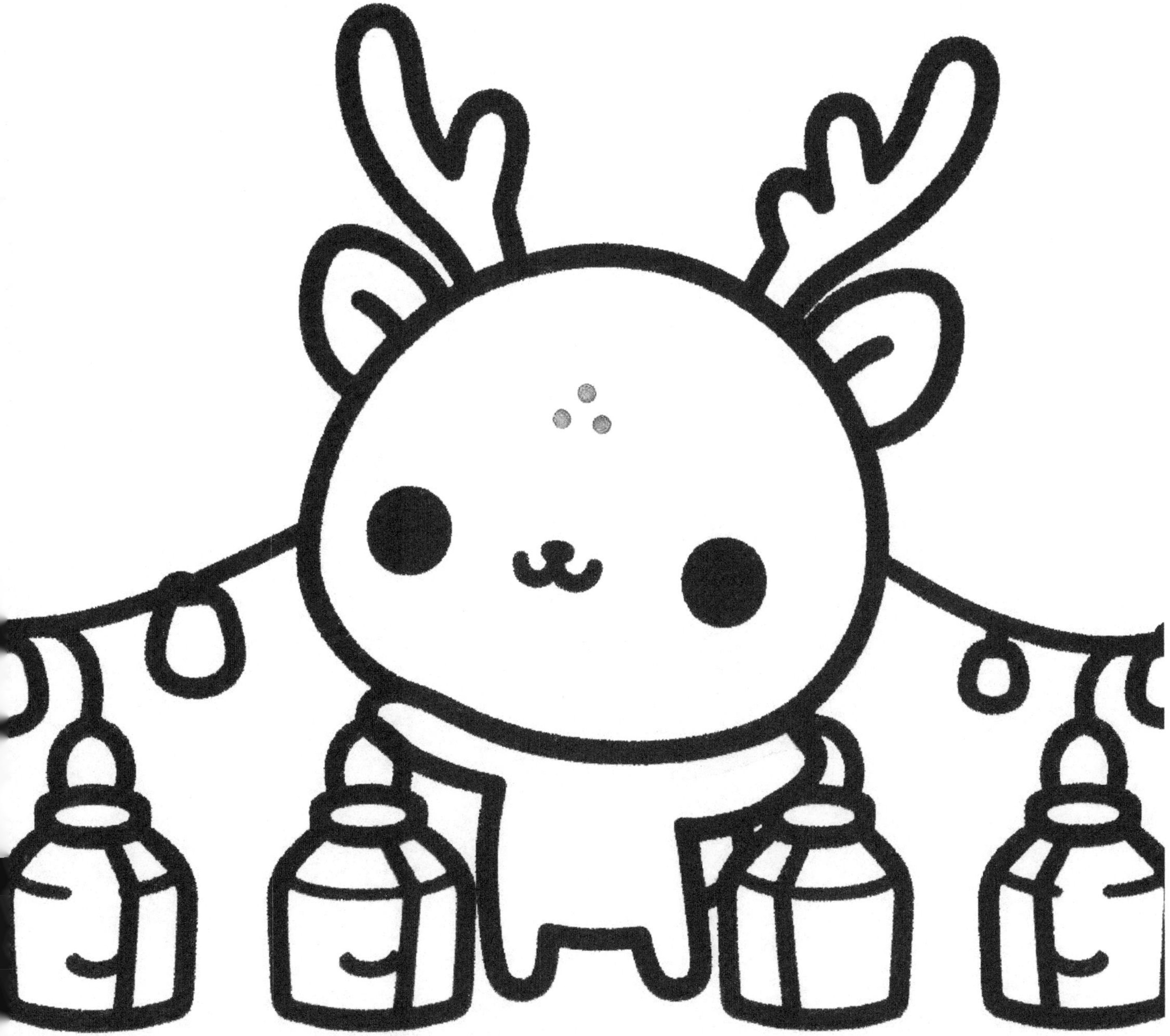

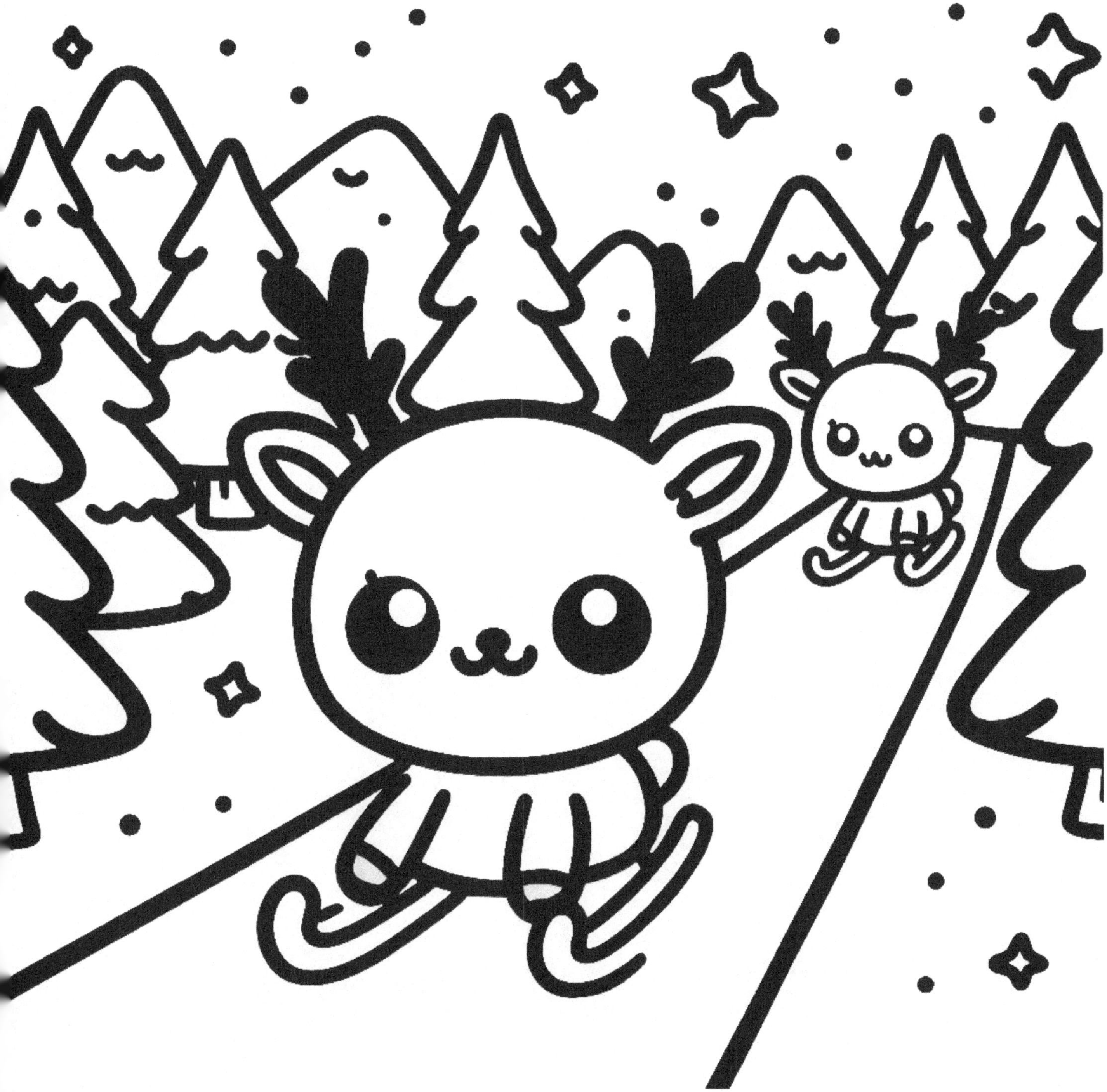

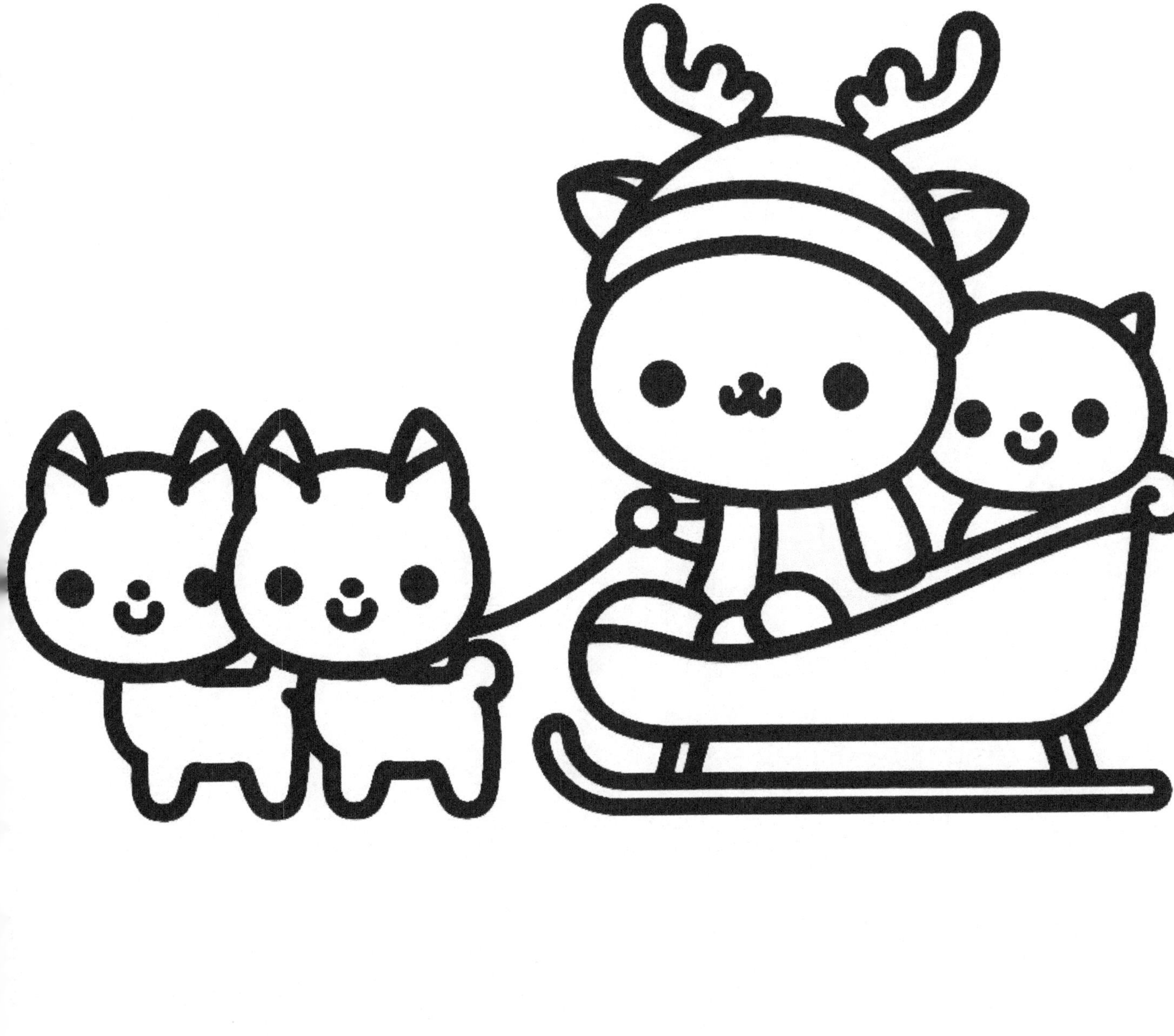

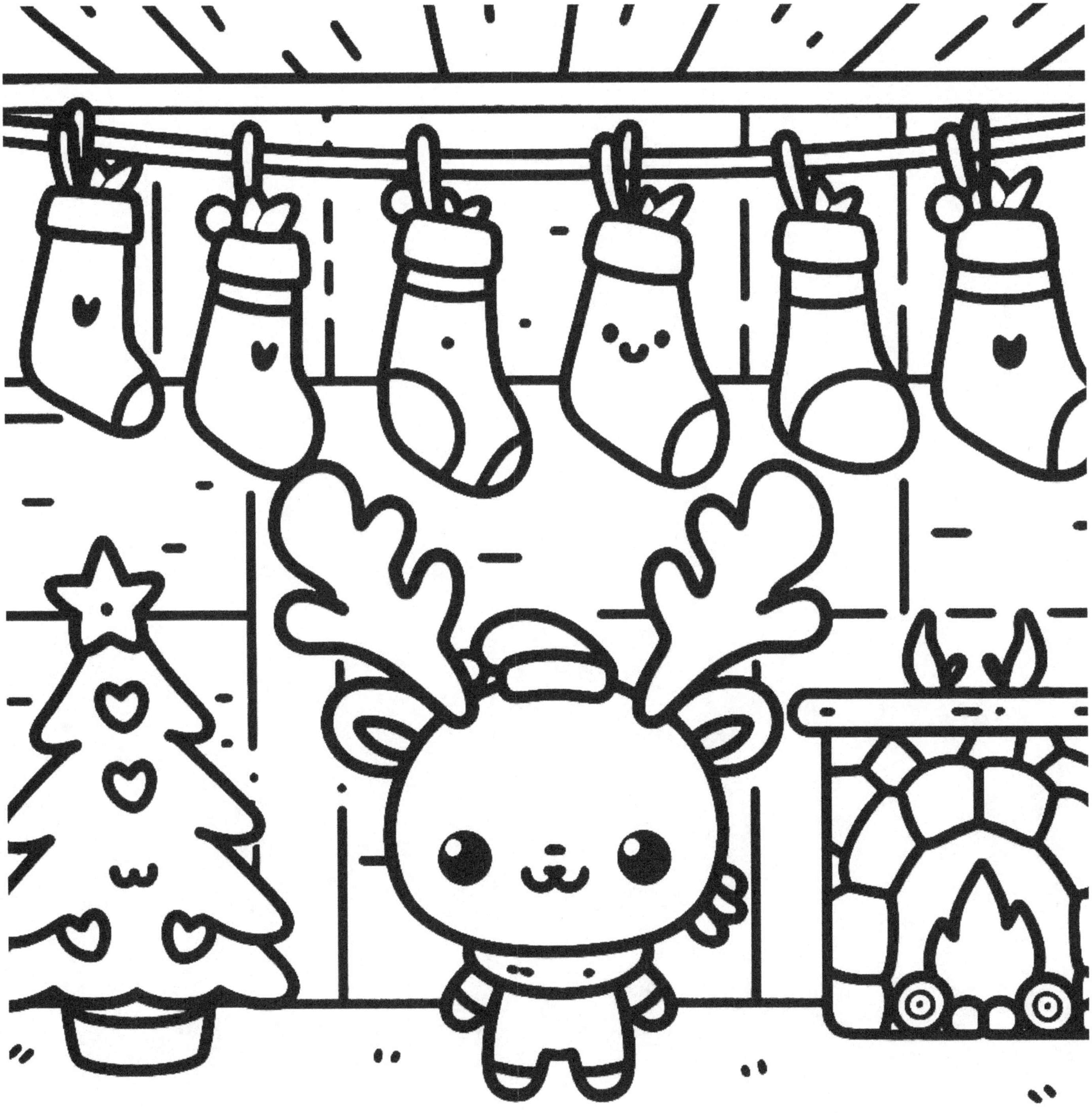

Coloring Guide Example

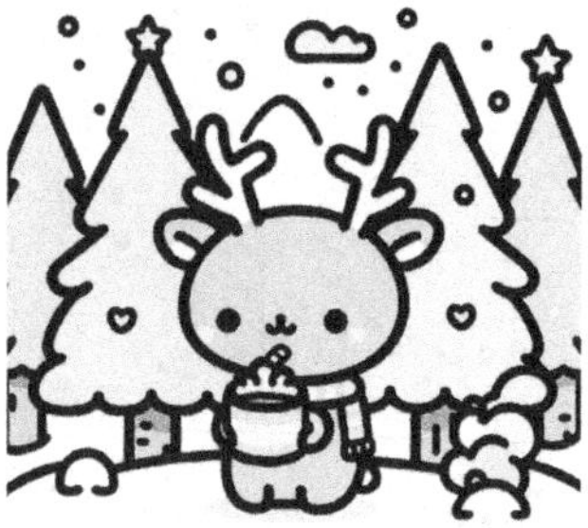
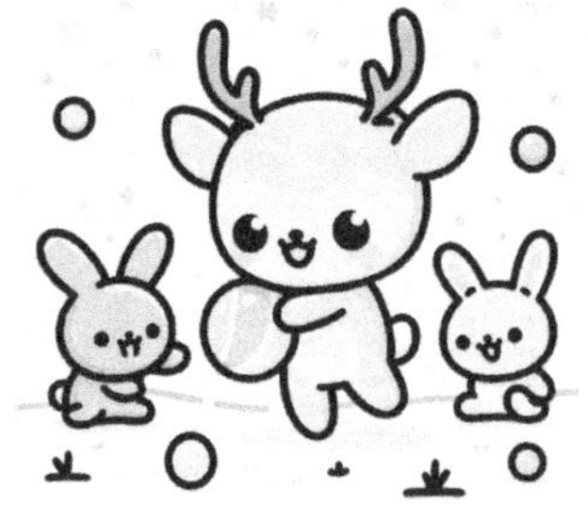
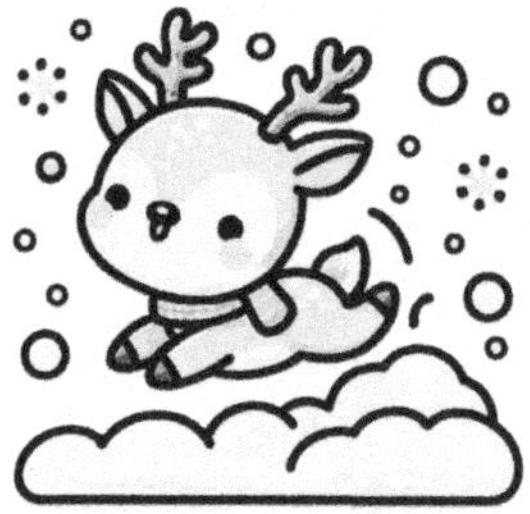
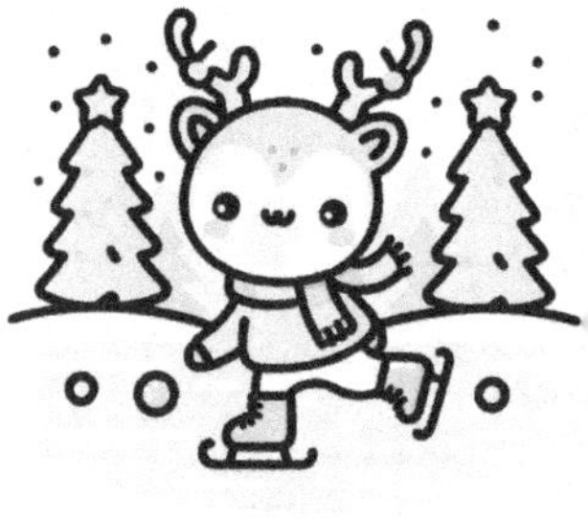
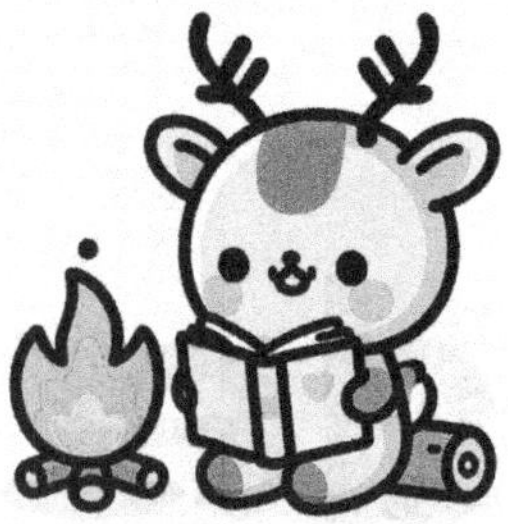
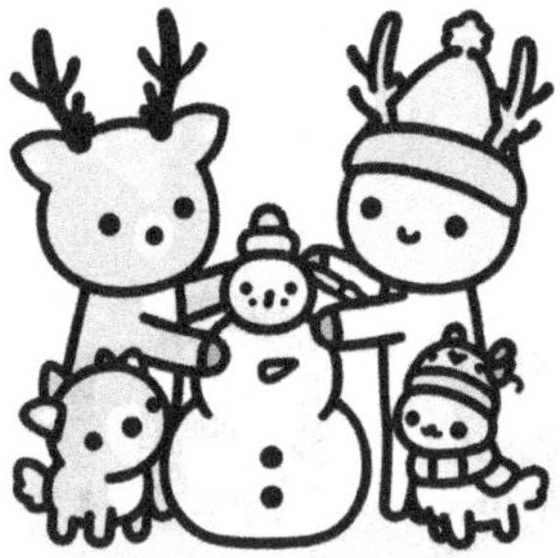
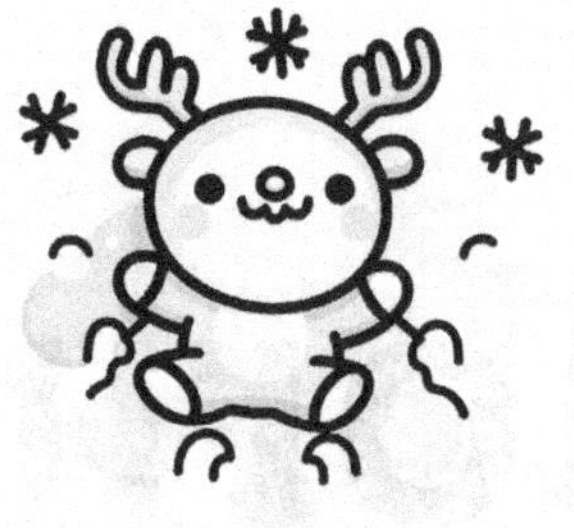
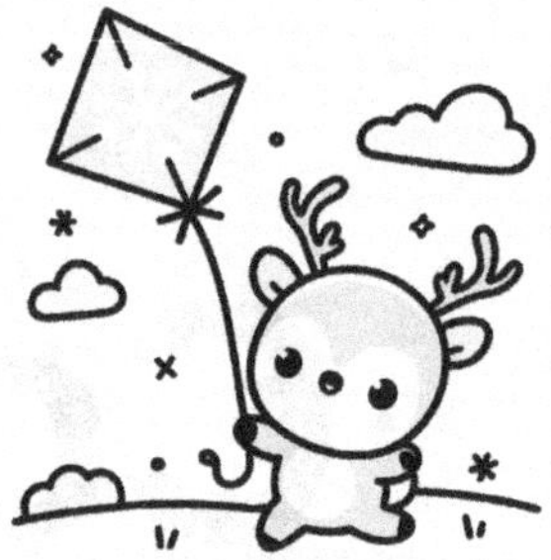

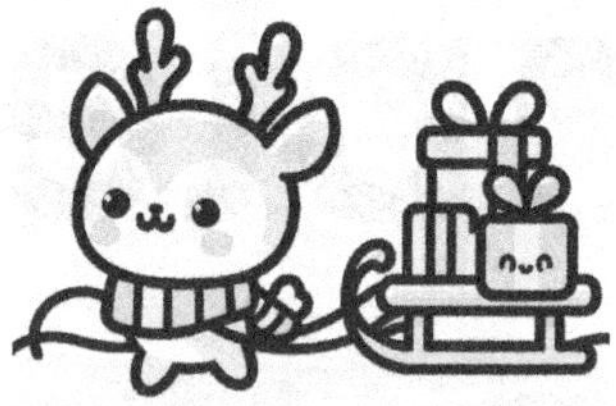
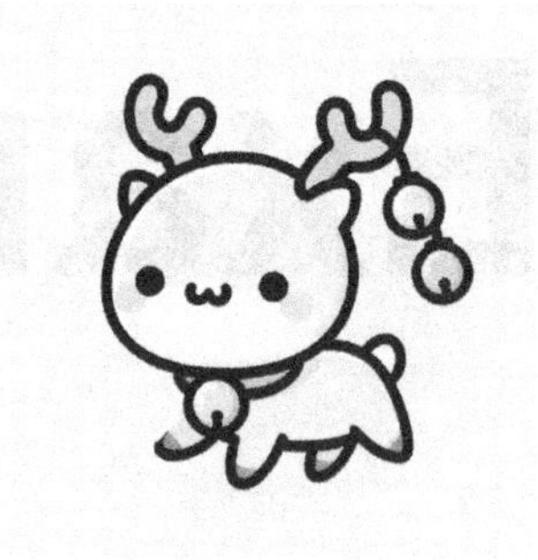
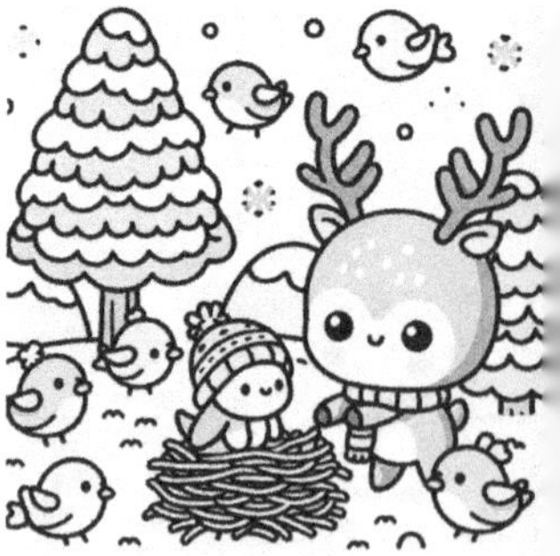
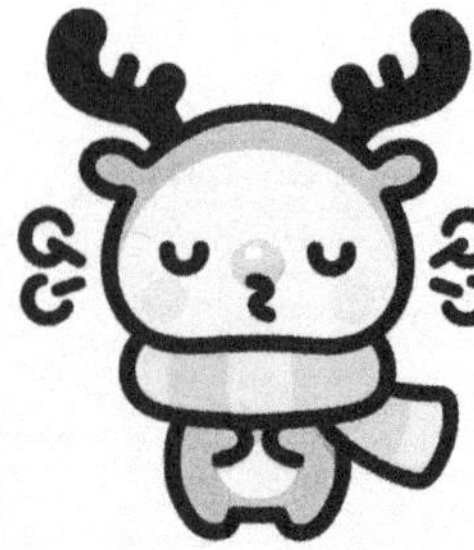
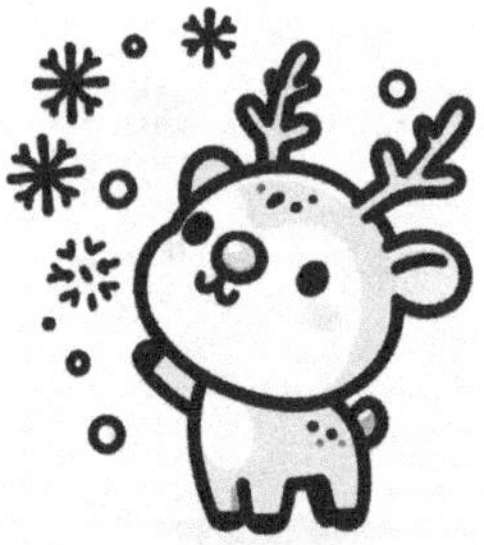
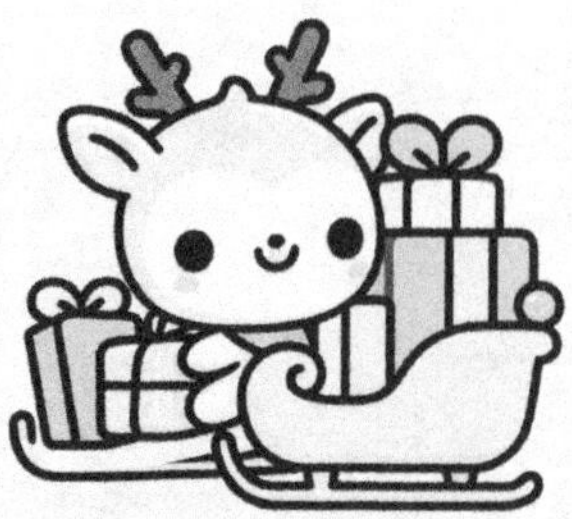
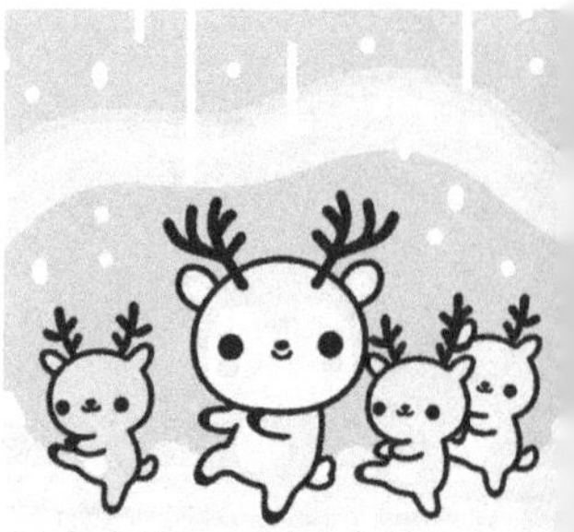

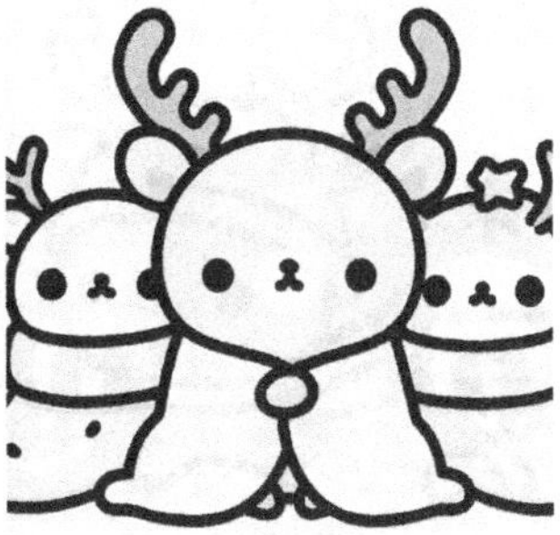
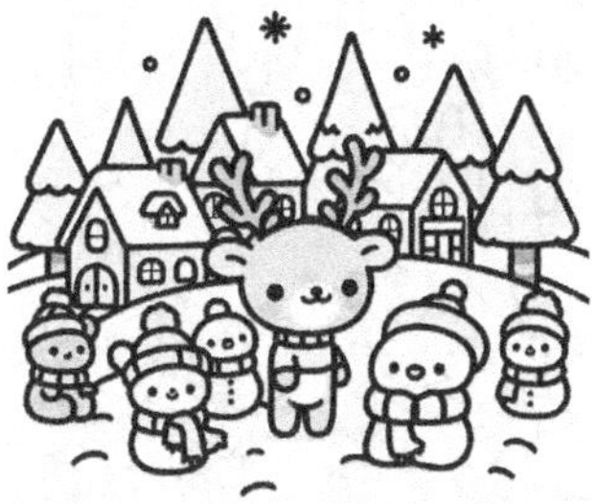
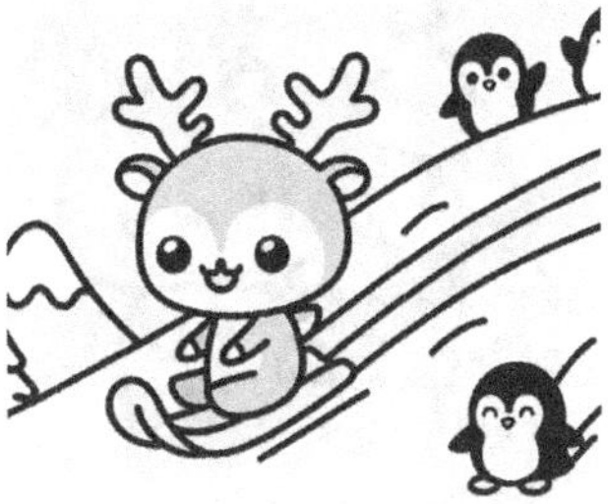
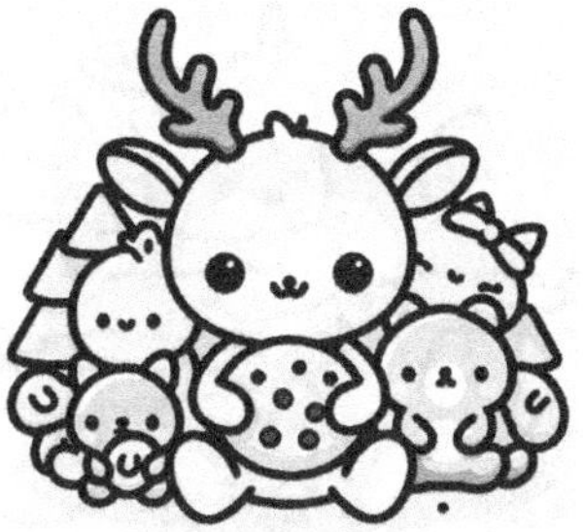
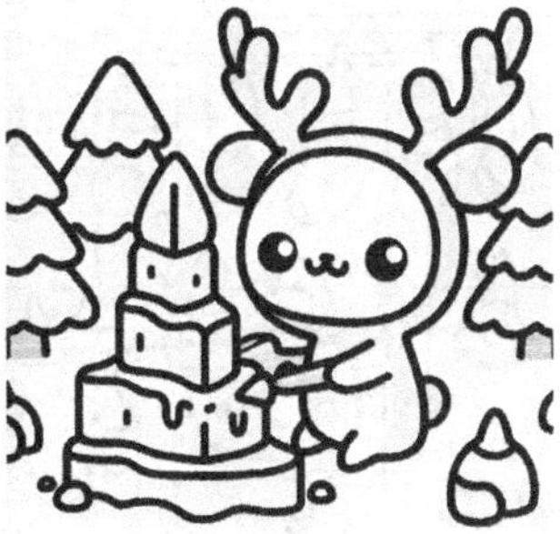
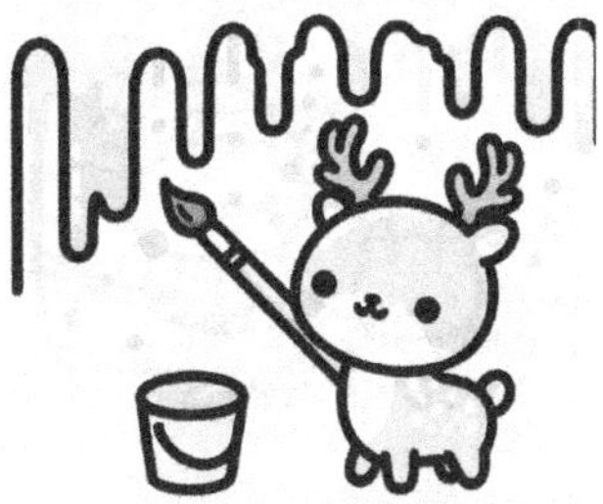
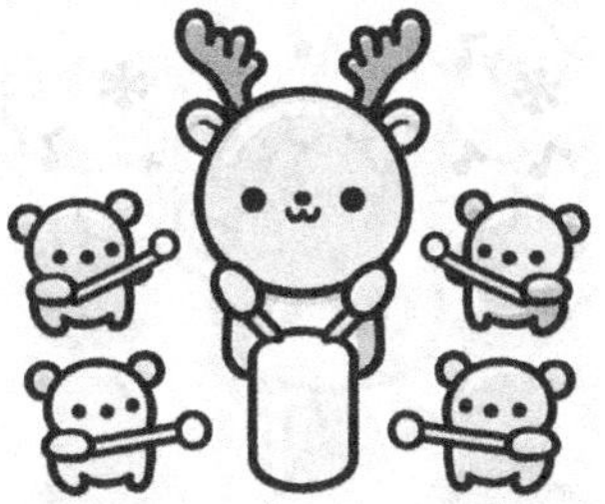
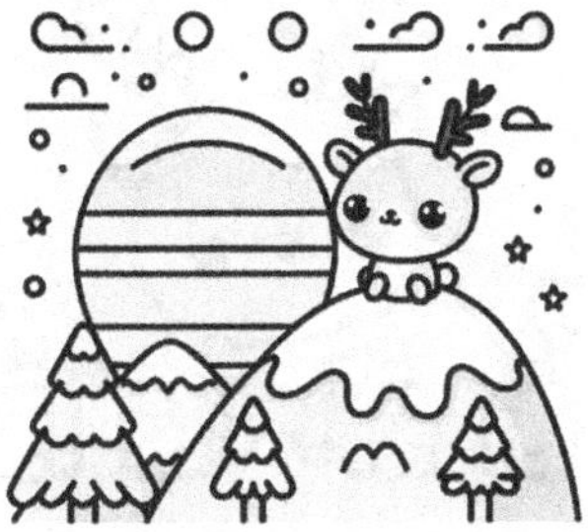
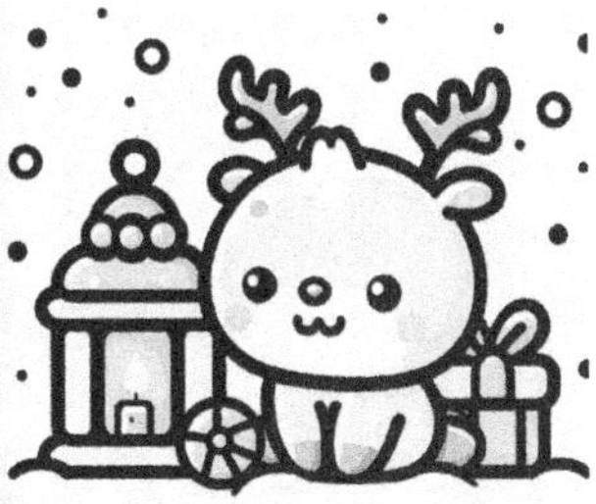
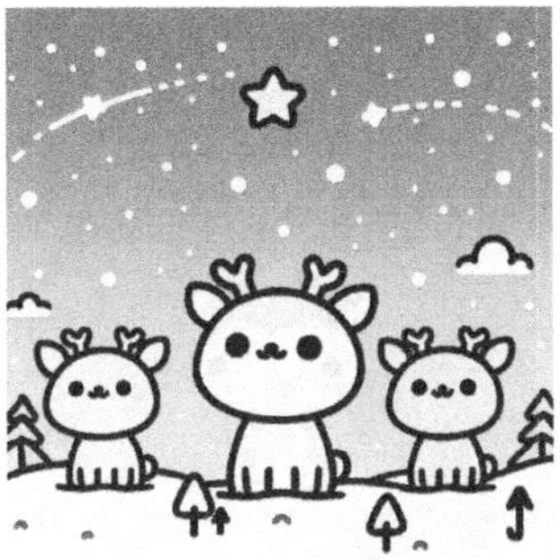
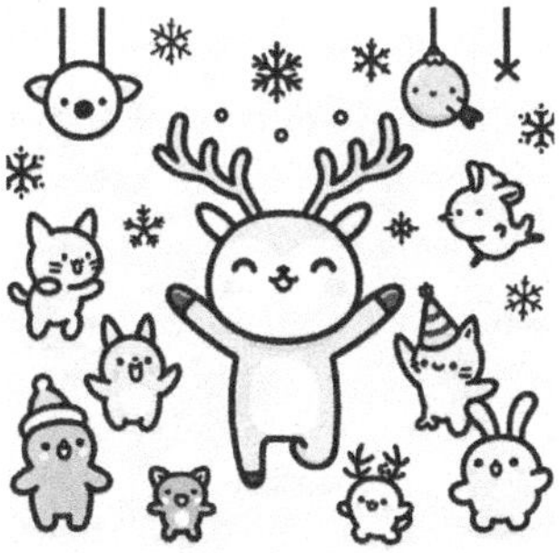
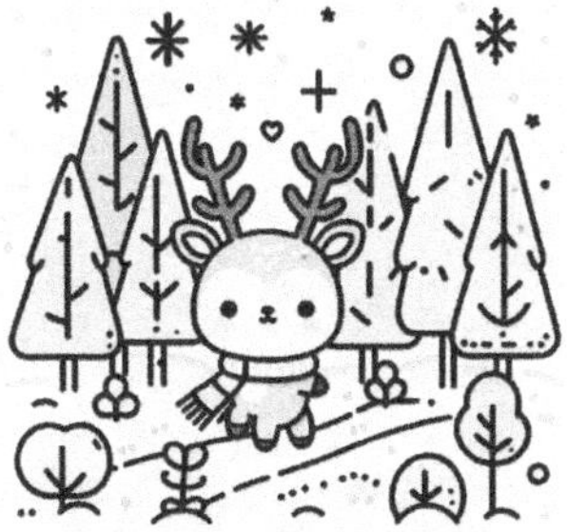
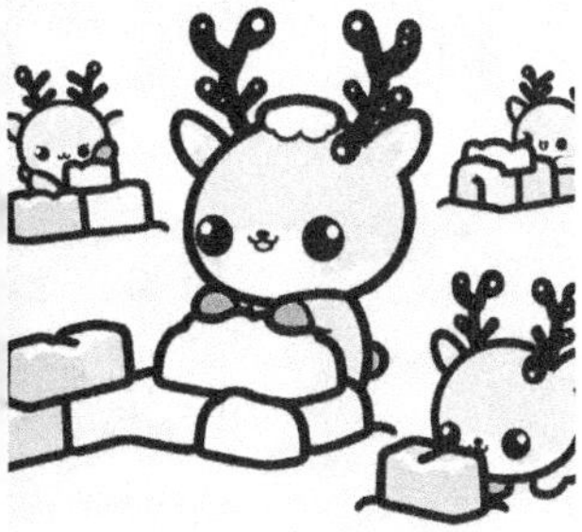
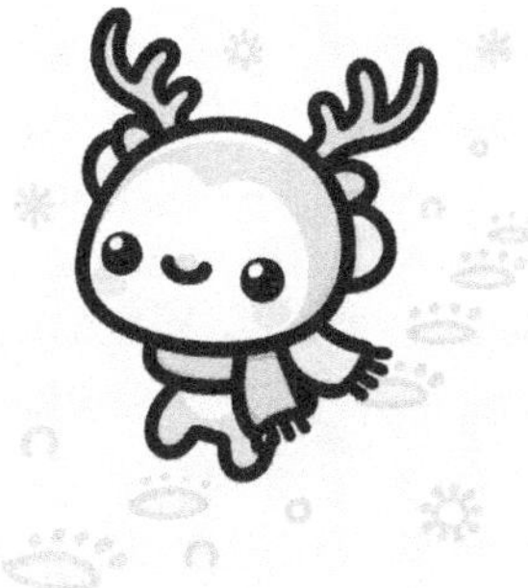
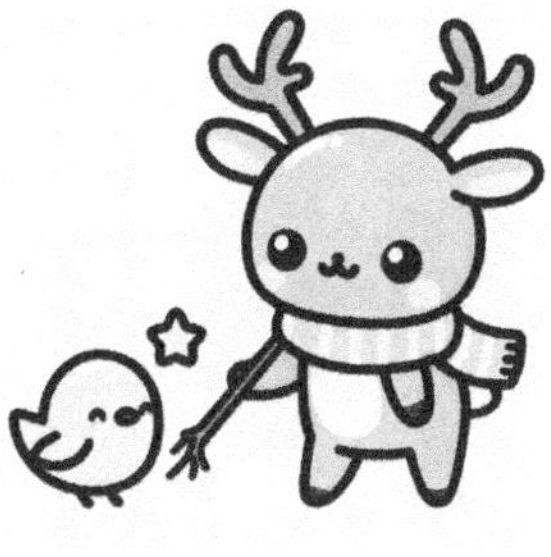
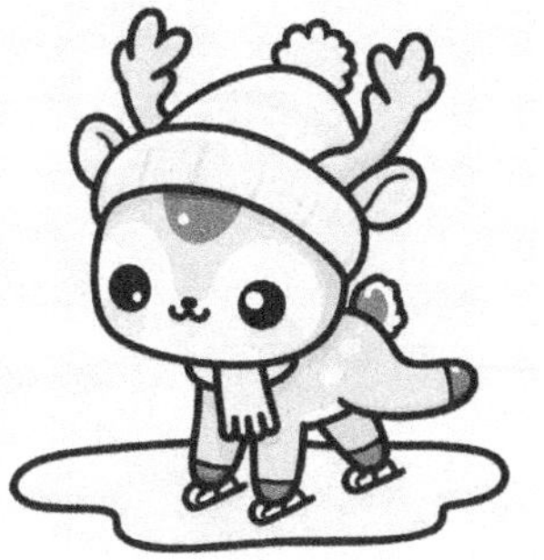

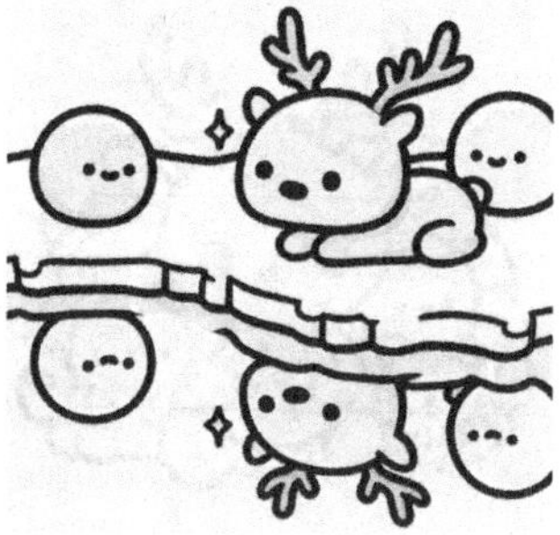
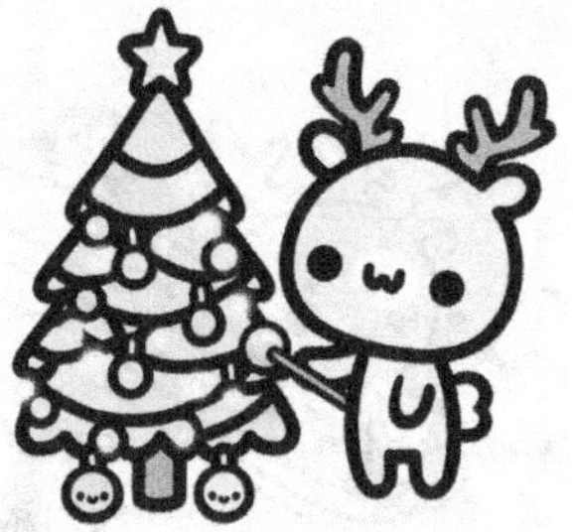
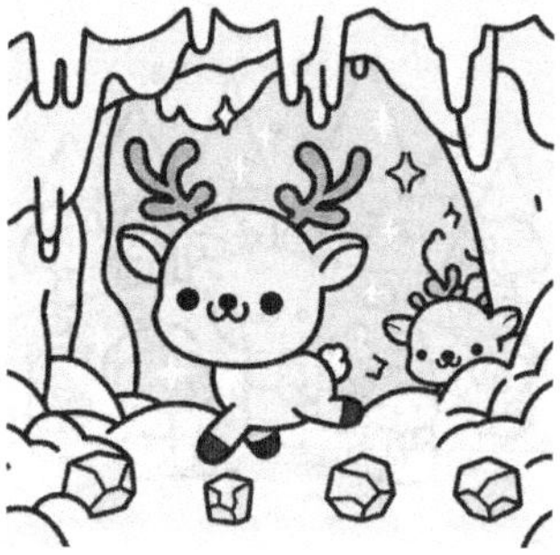
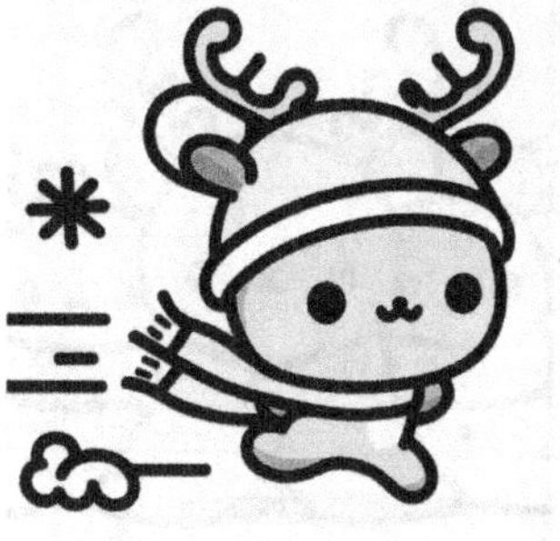
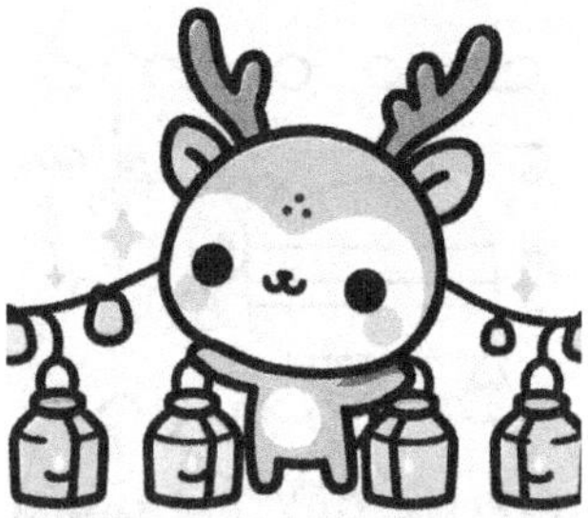
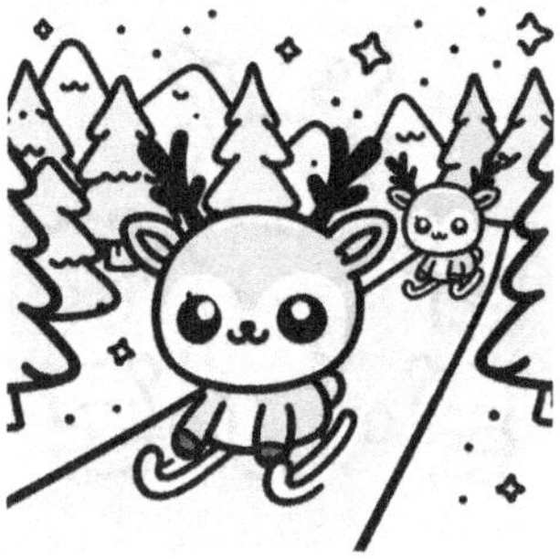
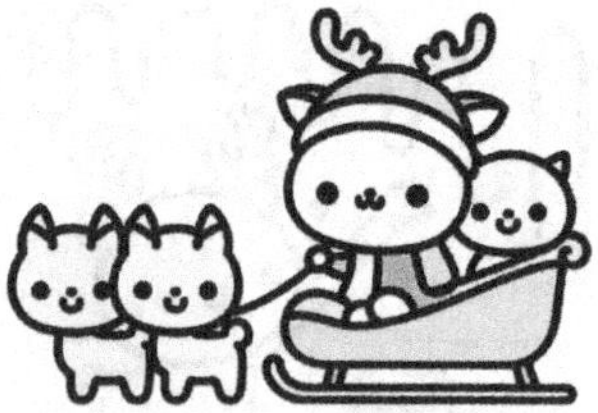
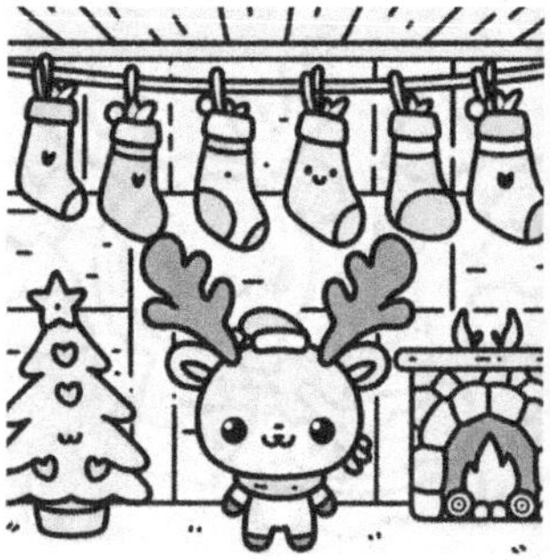

Made in the USA
Monee, IL
17 November 2024

70402696R00050